by
TOM
WILLIAMS

SWORD of the LORD
PUBLISHERS
P. O. BOX 1099, MURFREESBORO, TN 37133

Copyright 1988 by
Sword of the Lord Publishers

ISBN 0-87398-953-8

Second Printing: 1990

New Home of Tom Williams Ministries
Route 1, Box 133A
Koshkonong, MO 65692
417/264-7163

Printed and Bound in the United States of America

Dedication

Dedicated to my four wonderful children.
Thank you, Tim, Phyllis, Paul and Penny, for
your love, help and encouragement.

Acknowledgments

I take this opportunity and space to express my appreciation to my secretary, Sue Cawthron, for the many hours spent editing this book. I praise the Lord for her diligence and for the outstanding job that she did.

I also thank all who have prayed for and helped me, particularly during the last nine years as we faced many tomorrows in the trials of my wife's illness.

I owe a tremendous debt of gratitude to my family, to the pastors who have helped me and to the thousands of friends whom God has given us across America.

To Dr. Jack Hyles, I send a special "thank you" for the tremendous encouragement you have been to my heart.

Preface

I was just a young man when the Lord began to bring some heart-rending tomorrows into my life.

The road I have traveled as a Christian has led through valley after valley. But I have discovered, as did the psalmist David, that the Lord is with His children even in the valleys (Ps. 23). Although the valleys have been deep and long, my Saviour—the Lord Jesus Christ—was right there with me.

It is wonderful to have a High Priest who has compassion toward our infirmities, One who knows all about sorrow and grief. And He tells us in I Peter 5:7 to bring all our cares to Him.

I was grief-stricken in June, 1958, when my first wife passed away. That same year brought another time of great sorrow into my life as the Lord also called Home my little girl, born just a few days before my wife died. In a very real sense, as a young man I learned to commit my burdens to the Lord.

I suppose in a way these losses helped prepare me for the even greater trial I was to face several years later when my second wife contracted a very devastating disease, leaving her an invalid.

Through these and many other traumatic experiences, Isaiah 40:28-31 has been a tremendous pillar upon which I have leaned. God has used this passage to sustain me in a miraculous way:

"Hast thou not known? hast thou not heard, that the everlasting God, the Lord, the Creator of the ends of the earth, fainteth not, neither is weary? there is no searching of his *understanding. He giveth power to the faint; and to them that have no might he increaseth strength. Even the youths shall faint and be weary, and the young men shall utterly fall: But they that wait upon the Lord shall renew their strength; they shall mount up with wings as eagles; they shall run, and not be weary; and they shall walk, and not faint."*

I have found that God is capable not only of sustaining His people, but also of doing so in a far greater way than we can ask or even imagine (Eph. 3:20). And it has been because of the sustaining power of God in the midst of my hurts that I have been enabled to minister to others who are hurting.

Hundreds of thousands of people have heard the story of our testimony through my first book, *Twice Given for God's Glory,* through the recorded tapes, through our personal appearances, and on radio. As a result, I have had contact with literally thousands of hurting people through telephone calls, letters and personal visits.

It is with this thought in mind that I have written this book, *You Can Make It.* By revealing my heart in various situations, I felt perhaps I could encourage and, in a greater way, help others face whatever their tomorrows might bring.

As you read this book and in some measure walk the road with me, I trust you will sense God's presence as never before.

Contents

Preface

Acknowledgments

1 Beginning of Sorrows

"If I do not live through this childbirth, I want you and the children to live with my parents."

These were the words my wife spoke to me as we were driving to the hospital for the birth of our second child on May 21, 1958.

I was twenty-two years of age and Wanda was twenty-three. I remember saying to her that night, "Don't talk that way. You're just twenty-three years old; we still have our whole life ahead of us."

My thoughts went back to our wedding day on July 23, 1954. I remembered how pretty she looked and how proud I was that she was going to be my wife.

Wanda was 5'6" tall and weighed about 130 pounds. She was a beautiful brunette with a winning personality—always looking on the positive side of life. It just was not like Wanda to talk that way.

Perhaps God had impressed on her heart that she was going to die, but I tried to reassure her that everything would be all right.

The doctor had X-rayed her two weeks earlier and told me something seemed to be wrong with the baby, but he was not sure exactly what it was. He advised me not to tell Wanda about the problem, as it might really upset her. I followed his advice, but as I look back on that situation, I am not sure I did the right thing in keeping it from her.

The two weeks between the time of the X-rays and the time of birth were saturated with prayer. I prayed and cried to my Heavenly Father, asking Him to give Wanda and me the grace and strength to face whatever lay ahead.

As we drove on to the hospital that evening, I slipped my arm around Wanda's shoulder and drew her close, wanting to assure her that everything would be all right; yet at the same time, I was apprehensive about the possible problem with the baby.

Wanda labored for about eighteen hours, trying to give birth. When the doctor realized she just could not deliver, he again took X-rays. They revealed that the baby's head was twice as large as it should have been and that the baby had turned from the birth position back up to a sitting position in the womb. At that point he asked my permission to take the baby by Caesarean. A short while later our little girl, Sheryl Dee, was born.

Sheryl was a spina-bifida baby. She had a hole in her back about the size of a baseball. Her spine was split, and the spinal cord had pulled in and pinched. The lower portion of her body was paralyzed.

Except for the size of her head, the upper part of Sheryl's body functioned normally. Her arms moved freely, and her facial expressions were like those of any other newborn.

During the next few days I faced some of the most difficult moments I had ever experienced. I was the one who had to tell Wanda the condition of the baby and to break the news that Sheryl would not be coming home. I also had to tell her that the doctor said we could not have any more children.

Being a Christian for just two years, I found this a pretty choppy sea for a vessel so fragile. I am thankful that our Lord is the Master of the sea, and even to this young Christian He could speak, "Peace, be still."

Heartbroken but accepting it as the will of God, we decided we would adopt a baby later so our son Tim would not have to grow up as an only child. Even in the midst of tears and heartache, we both knew in our hearts that the Lord was in control.

The peace of God began to rule in our hearts as the Scripture says in Colossians 3:15; and we were able, by His grace, to control our emotions, even though our dreams had just been shattered . . . the dreams of all the things that go along with planning for the arrival of a precious baby.

We were thinking of the crib that we had fixed up—that would remain empty. What about all the cute things received at the baby shower? Could we bear to see the room that would have been Sheryl's? How would we feel when we saw other couples with their little ones? Many, many such thoughts flooded our minds.

But, praise God, He does not put more on us than we can bear! He often allows us to suffer and then gives grace and strength before a next trial. Little did I know this was just the beginning of sorrows, that soon the shadows would lengthen and the night would grow darker.

But God does not allow the floods to come and overwhelm us. Instead, He leads us gently into the river of life one step at a time to help prepare us for the floods. And He so graciously helped us that day.

After the peace of God had filled our hearts and enabled us to face Sheryl's condition, the doctor asked if I would take her to the General Hospital in Los Angeles. We lived in a suburb of Los Angeles, and our local hospital was not equipped to care for a baby in Sheryl's condition.

Tears streamed down my face as I placed our little daughter— just hours old—in the front seat of our car in a little receiving blanket, left my dear wife at the hospital and drove across the city to General Hospital

When I walked into the emergency entrance, I was shocked at what I saw. There were people lying everywhere. Some were on beds, some on hospital carts, some even on the floor.

Those who have never been inside a massive general hospital like the one in Los Angeles cannot imagine how I felt as I stood there and watched the constant flow of people coming in, in every imaginable kind of condition. Some had been shot, others stabbed; some were in the process of having babies.

The doctors and nurses were doing everything they could, but there just were not enough of them to take care of all the people.

This was where my little girl was going to live. I clutched Sheryl to my bosom and waited, almost hoping no one would help us. Finally a nurse came for Sheryl, explaining that the other hospital had called and told them I was coming.

I very carefully placed Sheryl in the nurse's arms and, with all the grace God had given me, leaned over and kissed our little girl good-bye.

Perhaps one of the hardest things I have ever done was to leave my precious baby in that massive hospital, but I knew it had to be done. God's grace was sufficient and His sustaining power evident. I felt those great everlasting arms enfold me and heard my Heavenly Father whisper, "Tom, you go on; I'll stay here and watch over her."

I was reassured then, as I am now, that He holds His great arms under us like the eagle holds its great wings under the eaglet, that He would encourage me in the heartaches and trials just as He had when things were going well. While driving back to the hospital to comfort my wife, I again committed everything to the Lord.

Wanda seemed to be doing fine after a few days, so the doctor released her. However, the day after she came home, she began to swell immensely. I called the doctor, and he called in a prescription for some water-reduction pills. He warned that she would have a sudden weight loss but that I should not be alarmed; the medication would be ridding her body of excess water.

The medicine made her violently ill. She was losing the pills almost as fast as I could give them to her. This went on throughout the day, so I called the doctor late that evening and told him her condition. He told me to call an ambulance and get her to the hospital immediately. That was on a Thursday evening.

The hospital doctors did everything they could for her, but nothing helped.

On Saturday afternoon the doctor said there was only a 50-50 chance of her living, that things were worsening all over her body and that a blood clot had formed in one of her lungs.

Wanda was very brave during the whole ordeal. This wonderful Christian kept wanting me to read to her. I knew the Beatitudes and Psalms would be a blessing so I read some of them to her. The Word of God was a great comfort. But as the night wore on, she became worse.

By Sunday morning the odds were 80-20 that she would not live. By now I was totally fatigued. I had been up day and night, going back and forth between the two hospitals, trying to find out how the baby was doing and spending as much time as possible by Wanda's bedside.

Our faithful pastor, Rev. Raymond Overstreet of Norwalk, California, stood by me and literally slept at the hospital. Such a comfort it was to have a pastor standing by in our hour of trial! Other Christian friends came and prayed and tried to comfort us. And, of course, the blessed Holy Spirit was such a wonderful Comforter.

I shall always remember Sunday, June 8, 1958, for that

day God spoke to my heart and asked if I was willing to let Wanda go.

I remember going out to my car—a 1955 Chevrolet—and kneeling in the back floorboard. There on my knees I surrendered all I had to my Heavenly Father—my wife, our two-year-old son Tim and our baby girl—telling Him that, if He wanted to take Wanda, I was willing to release her.

While I was on my knees in the car, the Lord gave me just a glimpse of how Abraham must have felt when God asked him to give up Isaac (Gen. 22:1-14). The Lord was not asking Abraham for his cattle, sheep, camels, tents or lands; He was asking for his dearly beloved son!

In the car that day, the Lord was separating my own flesh from me. I went through a battle before yielding to His will. In a very small way, it was almost as though I was walking through Gethsemane with my Saviour. I so greatly wanted to pray that He would let my wife live and be whole. But I knew that I had to come to the place where I could say and mean it, "Not my will, but thine be done."

Hundreds of thoughts came to mind as I pondered how different everything would be without Wanda. How would I tell my little boy that neither his baby sister nor his mother would be coming home? How would he react? What would the house be like without Wanda's love, her singing, her laughter, her cooking and her greeting each time I came home? Who would help me bear the burden of Sheryl's illness? Could I face tomorrow with no one to share my life?

Then the blessed Holy Spirit began flooding my heart with the things I had learned from the Scriptures. "I will never leave thee, nor forsake thee" (Heb. 13:5). "Yea, though I walk through the valley of the shadow of death, I will fear no evil: for thou art with me; thy rod and thy staff they comfort me" (Ps. 23:4).

Assured once again of God's promises and comfort, I got up and went back into the hospital around 2:00 p.m. As I walked toward the room, a nurse met me at the door. She put her arm around me and pleaded, "Mr. Williams, *please* don't go in that room. Your wife just passed away after going into convulsions. You would not want to see what you would see if you went in there now."

I waited until the doctors had straightened out her body and made her as presentable as possible. The convulsions had twisted her body and distorted her face.

Still somewhat dazed, I went downstairs and told her parents and her brother that God had called Wanda Home.

The doctor offered his sympathy, explaining that he had done all he knew to do. Then he asked permission to perform an autopsy to determine why Wanda's body had not responded to any medication. That was a difficult decision to make at that time since I was physically and emotionally exhausted. I reasoned, "What difference does it make *why* she died? The fact is, my wife is dead!"

But when he explained that it might save someone else's life, I consented to the autopsy. I was thankful I did, as they discovered that Wanda's kidneys had totally failed. After completing the autopsy, they asked Wanda's parents if she had ever fallen or received a blow on her back which could have damaged her kidneys. In thinking back to her childhood, they remembered that when she was a little girl she had fallen out of a barn.

I was glad I had allowed the autopsy because when most of us lose a loved one, we have a tendency to wonder if there was something we could have done to prevent death, some way we could have helped more—when, in reality, we were in no way to blame for what happened.

Breaking the News to Tim

Grief stricken, I prayed for strength to break the news to my little boy and explain to him that he and Daddy would have to face tomorrow without a mommy and without a sweetheart.

I hardly knew where to start. How could I explain to a little two-and-one-half-year-old that he no longer had a mommy? The one who had been with him day and night. The one who had nursed him, changed his diapers and watched him sit up for the first time. The one who had helped him take his first steps, laughed at his wobbly legs and so tenderly sung him to sleep at night. The one who had played with him each day while I was at work. The one who had taught him how to talk. How could I help him know that she had not just gone to the store or to visit someone? How could I help him remember her and yet forget her so that life could go on?

I did not know the answers to all these questions, but in the midst of my trial-filled tomorrows, which began at twenty-two years of age, I have learned that trials work in one of two ways: they can draw us closer to the Lord, or they can make us bitter. How sad when folks cannot see that God has nothing but the very best in mind for them! He is the Master Designer who wants to fashion us like unto Himself.

Romans 8:28 does not say that all things are good, but it does say that "all things work together for good to them that love God, to them who are the called according to his purpose."

This reminds me of my mother's biscuits. She made them from "scratch." By themselves, the different ingredients that go into a biscuit do not taste very good. But when they are properly measured and blended together, they work together for good, and the result is a pan full of delicious biscuits.

In a similar way, God takes what we call the tragedies of our lives and turns them into tremendous blessings to us as well as to others.

So in facing our tomorrows, we can remember the words of the songwriter: "Many things about tomorrow I don't seem to understand. But I know who holds tomorrow, and I know who holds my hand" (from "I Know Who Holds Tomorrow" by Ira Stanphill).

As I made funeral arrangements, I was keenly aware that God knew my tomorrows, that He held my hand. So I leaned the more heavily on the Lord and drew from His wisdom and strength. Truly, God was and still is "a very present help in trouble" (Ps. 46:1). I learned that God is not a long way off and that He does not take a long time to hear our prayers!

In addition to deciding which casket to use, what clothing Wanda would wear and what the order of service should be, I also had to make some decisions concerning my young son and myself. Should we continue to live in California? Should we move back to my native state of Texas? All of my relatives were there, and certainly they would be a comfort to me. However, Wanda had requested that the children and I live with her parents if she died.

If I granted her request, then which cemetery should I bury her in? If we were moving to Texas, should I bury her there? Could the baby be transferred from Los Angeles to Texas in her condition? Would the hospital there be equipped to care for her? Would it devastate my wife's folks to have me move away and take their grandchildren?

These and other thoughts tumbled through my mind, but I was wonderfully comforted by my Saviour's invitation in Matthew 11:28-30:

"Come unto me, all ye that labour and are heavy laden, and I will give you rest. Take my yoke upon you, and learn of me; for I am meek and lowly in heart: and ye shall find rest unto your souls. For my yoke is easy, and my burden is light."

The Lord's comfort extended beyond the funeral and strengthened me day after day as I fought the loneliness of losing my dear wife, leaving me with empty arms, an empty bed, an empty house. He also comforted me each day as I made my way across Los Angeles to the General Hospital to be with my little girl, who was slowly dying. Each day as I went, I can remember praying for strength, grace and mercy to face however many tomorrows Sheryl and I might have together. Sheryl's head was growing rapidly, but there was nothing the doctors could do for her.

Leaving the General Hospital each day, I drove home and tried to fill in as both Mama and Daddy to little Tim. Of course, he was too young to understand all that was happening, and night after night I let him get in bed with me so I could comfort him as he cried for his mother.

We granted my wife's request to live with her parents, so Tim and I stayed there until I remarried. Grandma Claud was a wonderful help during those long months. And even though she could not replace Tim's mother, she tried so very hard to make life easier for both Tim and me.

Little Sheryl lived four months and twenty days after Wanda's death. Her head had grown to be the same length as her body—almost twenty-one inches long. She was not at all pleasant to look at; yet, God gave me a tremendous love for her.

Through this experience with Sheryl, God taught me how much He really loved me and how I ought to love sinners and win them, through love, to the Lord Jesus Christ.

One day as I was sitting by her bedside, I reached through the rails of the bed. As she grasped my fingers with her tiny hand, God spoke to my heart and said, "Tom, she's really ugly, isn't she?"

Startled, I replied, "Yes, Sir, she is."

He said, "But don't you love her?"

I told Him, "Oh, yes! Very, very much!"

He asked, "Do you love her as much as you love Tim?"

I thought for awhile and then replied, "Yes, I believe I do—maybe even a little more."

Then He said, "Tom, I'm going to take Sheryl Home soon. But I want you to always remember what she looks like because that's what *you* looked like when I loved you."

And for the first time in my life, my spiritual eyes were opened to the reality of what Romans 5:8 *really* meant: "But God commendeth his love toward us, in that, while we were yet sinners, Christ died for us."

Then I realized that God had loved me when I was made ugly by sin, when sin had wrecked my life and almost ruined it.

That day with Sheryl, God told me, "Tom, always remember that. Always remember the pit from which you were digged and how I loved you while you were still an unsaved sinner."

I thank God for the tremendous spiritual lesson He taught me from little Sheryl's physical condition. My Heavenly Father looked down past a lot of tomorrows and knew that less than three years from that time He would call me from being a salesman into the ministry of an evangelist. The lesson He taught me at the bedside of little Sheryl has been invaluable in my twenty-six years of evangelism.

How many times I have been reminded of that experience and have been able, through the power and grace of God, to continue to reach out to people in their sin and bring them to Christ!

I remember a man at a street meeting I was holding in Sacramento, California. He was so drunk he could hardly stand upright. His clothes were filthy, his beard was matted, and his body odor was so bad it almost took my breath. The Lord asked me, "Tom, do you love him?"

My mind went back to the lesson He taught me that day in the hospital with Sheryl, and I replied, "Yes, Sir, I do."

Then He said, "Help him to know Me."

I led the man over to the curb and helped him sit down. I bowed my head and prayed, "Father, if I am to win him, You must sober him."

Almost before I was through praying, the man was sober. I began talking to him, and within a half hour he had confessed the Lord Jesus Christ as his Saviour.

Again the Lord asked me if I really loved him, and I said, "Yes, Sir, I do."

Then He said, "Take him and clean him up."

So I took him to the rescue mission and bathed him, shaved him and put a suit of clothes on him that I got from the mission.

The Lord asked again, "Tom, do you really love him?"

And I said, "Yes, Sir, I do."

The Lord then told me to get him to his family. I asked the man if he knew where they were. He told me where they lived and said he wanted to go home. I took him to the bus station and bought a ticket. Several weeks passed. One day I received a letter from his wife. She wrote:

> I may never meet you this side of Heaven, but what you have done for us is beyond words.
> I had not seen or heard from my husband in over six years. I did not know if he was dead or alive. Now we are a family again, and he and the children and I are all going to church together faithfully.

I bowed my head and thanked my Heavenly Father that He had taught me to love the unlovely through one of my tomorrows.

Sheryl Goes Home

Not long after the experience at Sheryl's bedside, I received a call from General Hospital about three o'clock one morning, telling me that Sheryl had passed away.

Little did I know the far-reaching effects of the lesson God taught me that day. It was as though God had brought little Sheryl into the world and allowed her to live just long enough to accomplish His purpose. Then He took her Home.

We made the funeral arrangements, and little Sheryl was buried about twenty-five feet north of her mother's grave.

I'll never forget that day. Just as the graveside ceremony was ending and we were about to lower the tiny casket into the grave, I heard a man screaming. He was lying on the ground in the cemetery, pulling up handfuls of grass.

I walked from the graveside of my daughter and knelt beside the man, asking if there was anything I could do. Through his tears, he replied, "You don't understand! You don't understand! My wife is under this piece of grass!"

I said, "I believe I understand. My wife is under that section over there, and we're just putting my little baby girl in that open grave."

He sat up with a shocked look on his face and asked, "Man, how can you stand it?"

I began telling him about the Lord Jesus Christ and how He had saved me—a drunkard and pornography pusher—at almost twenty-one years of age. I told him that God had wonderfully worked in my life, and I shared with him some of the blessings God had given me. It was thrilling to see him suddenly grow quiet, enabling me to present to him the wonderfulness of the Lord Jesus Christ.

In the midst of all the trials and heartaches with Wanda and Sheryl, I learned that there are tremendous blessings and great lessons to be learned. God truly does enable us to face our tomorrows.

2 The Search

After Wanda's death, I deeply longed for companionship. Out of the loneliness of my heart, I cried out to God for a helpmeet—someone who would love Tim as her own child and who would love me and stand by my side, someone to help heal my broken heart and to fill the emptiness of both our lives.

I have talked with folks who have lost a husband or wife, and many felt they would be showing disloyalty to their deceased loved one if they were to remarry. I searched my own heart and felt peace that Wanda would not want me to spend the rest of my life without someone to share my love.

I knew that to remarry would not mean I was being disloyal to Wanda, whom I had loved very dearly. But in order for me to successfully go through the healing process, I had to accept the fact that my loved one was dead. I had to seek once again for a sense of fulfillment in my life and begin to meet the needs that were still in my heart.

Throughout the Word of God, the replacement principle is taught. We find this in Romans 12:2, "Be not conformed to this world: but be ye transformed by the renewing of your mind."

A person cannot just take out the bad thoughts and vain imaginations; he must replace them with holy thoughts and think on right things.

The Apostle Paul admonishes us in Philippians 4:8, "Finally, brethren, whatsoever things are true, whatsoever things are honest, whatsoever things are just, whatsoever things are pure, whatsoever things are lovely, whatsoever things are of good report; if there be any virtue, and if there be any praise, think on these things."

Even so, when something precious is taken from us, such as a wife, child, husband, parent or someone else, it is wise to practice the replacement principle. This is not to say we are replacing that person—no one could ever do that—but we must fill the emptiness with something or someone that will strengthen and encourage us to be happy and useful. With this thought in mind, I began to ask the Lord for one who would make me a more complete, more fulfilled person.

I wondered what kind of person God would send to help fill the void in my life and in Tim's. Would she be short or tall? A blonde, a brunette, a redhead, or would she have jet-black hair? What kind of personality would she have?

It goes without saying that the number one requirement would be that she love the Lord Jesus Christ. Then she must love me enough to love my son. She would have to step into the life of a three-year-old boy and win his heart and love, realizing that to love me was to love my son. This was especially important because I did not want a stepmother/stepson image in her life or his. I felt sure that when I remarried, we would have other children, and I wanted them to be equally loved by both of us.

Then, too, I had to consider my first wife's folks in choosing a new mother for their grandson, realizing that she would be stepping in and fulfilling the duties their daughter would have fulfilled. Also, my new wife's parents would become grandparents immediately. Would they love Tim and take him into their hearts as a real grandchild, too?

I wondered if I could love another wife like I should and not compare her to Wanda. Could I really let go of the past and look to the future? Would I be able to let another woman discipline Tim without interfering? So many thoughts filled my mind so as to almost overwhelm me. I realized there was no way that I could, in myself, find someone to meet our needs in all these areas.

I cried out to my Heavenly Father, asking Him to find this unique individual. Little did I know how perfectly my Father already was preparing a young lady to meet these vast needs.

One day Tim asked if we could visit his Uncle E. B., my first wife's brother. He and his wife had children about Tim's age, and Tim wanted to play with his cousins. I had no idea that the Lord was using this to introduce me to my future wife.

E. B. at that time was working with the American Sunday School Union. He was a part of their rural ministry of establishing Sunday schools in out-of-the-way places. In the summertime he would have about sixteen Vacation Bible Schools. Christian young people from all over southern California would volunteer to work with him and other missionaries. I did not know that a young lady had come to live with his family for the summer to help in his work.

When Tim and I walked into E. B.'s home, there stood a beautiful young girl. The Lord told me then that she was the girl He wanted me to marry. I immediately questioned: "But, Father, she's so young." He replied, "Tom, if you don't want the one I have for you, then you may find your own." Needless to say, without any further argument, I set out to win her heart.

It didn't take long that afternoon to learn that she was only sixteen years of age. Pamela Marie James was from a small town about one hundred miles east of Los Angeles. Pam came from a fine Christian home and was the oldest of three girls. She and her family attended the First Baptist Church of Hemet, California.

I had known Pam only a couple of hours when the mailman came, bringing her a twenty-five-page letter from her boyfriend. I thought, *This must be serious; that is more than I would write in **twenty** letters!* I believe that letter would have been enough to discourage me had I not known the Lord wanted me to marry Pam.

When I told her that weekend what the Lord had told me about her, she immediately replied, "I don't understand all that's happening, but when you walked in the door today and your eyes met mine, I knew you were the man I was going to marry!"

I asked Pam if I could come back the next weekend to see if our feelings were as strong for each other after we had been apart for a week. So Tim and I made another visit the next week. When we left that time, I told Pam I thought we should wait two months. If she still wanted me to come and if I still felt the same toward her, I would drive to Hemet and see her, as she would be back home by then, and I would be meeting her parents.

I don't need to tell you that I experienced a lot of anxiety during those next two months. I knew that if I had been in the situation of Pam's folks, and a twenty-three-year-old man with a young son wanted to date my sixteen-year-old daughter, I too would have a lot of questions.

The two months dragged by, and with each passing day I knew beyond doubt that I loved Pam.

When I picked up the telephone to call and see if she wanted me to come, I had mixed emotions. In my heart I knew she was the one the Lord had chosen to be my wife, but in my flesh I was sure that either Pam, her parents or both would tell me not to come. Above all of my desires, I wanted to do what was right.

When Pam answered and we had exchanged greetings, I asked to speak to her dad. I told him I realized that because of the big age difference between Pam and me and because I was a widower with a young son, he and Mrs. James had a lot to take into consideration. After we had talked for awhile,

he invited me to come and see Pam and to meet them
personally.

Pam and I spent the entire day with her parents, going over
my situation. They told me that I could date Pam that evening
and that, if we decided marriage was the will of God for our
lives, we would have their blessings.

Pam and I spent the evening sitting in the car reading the
Bible, praying and talking. I tried to impress upon Pam that I
was not just some guy looking for a date, that I was searching
for a wife for myself and a mother for Tim. I told her there would
never be a honeymoon cottage for just two. I wanted her to
realize she would be a mother instantly. I explained to her my
concerns (which I mentioned earlier in this chapter), since she
needed to know fully what she was getting into; it wouldn't work
any other way.

Naturally, I asked her about the boy who had written the
twenty-five-page letter. She assured me that the Lord had
removed him from her life and had given me her heart.

When the evening had ended, we had absolute peace that
we were to marry when she graduated from high school the
following summer.

I drove back to Los Angeles that night, praising God for the
way He was taking care of my tomorrows.

3 The Courtship

I could hardly wait for each weekend to come. I would drive to Pam's house on Friday night and stay until Sunday morning. Her parents were very gracious and allowed me to sleep on the hide-a-bed in the living room.

Mr. James worked long hours driving a Helms bread truck, so there were many things he did not have time to do. Since they allowed me to stay there each weekend, I tried to show my appreciation by working around the home. I chopped wood for the fireplace, painted the exterior of the house, mowed grass, cleaned his truck and gathered the fruit from their fruit trees. I would tease Mr. James, telling him that he was Laban and I was Jacob, working to get Rachel. How I praise the Lord I didn't have to wait seven years! Not because of the work but because of my love for Pam.

Pam and I tried to put variety into our dating time. Sometimes we would drive up to the mountains at Idylwild or to Big Bear where we would hike and have picnics. At other times we would go to some of the many amusements in southern California. The ocean was a favorite for both of us. We liked to sit and watch the waves break along the shore or watch a pelican diving for a fish. Pam was so mature for her age and knew so much of God's Word that we spent hours fellowshiping in the Scriptures. She could quote hundreds of verses, including the entire book of Romans. We went to youth rallies and different meetings where I was speaking as a layman.

Each Sunday I would leave Hemet early in the morning and drive back to my local church, where I was Sunday school superintendent.

About three months after our courtship began, I tenderly placed an engagement ring on Pam's left hand. The next day her youngest sister ran down their street, shouting, "Pam has a ring! Pam has a ring!"

After we were engaged, I took Tim on some of our dates. I told him I wanted him to start calling Pam "Mother." I was not sure how this was going to work out. I knew it would be a real test when Pam would come to Los Angeles, where I was living with my first wife's folks, and Tim would call her Mother. However, Wanda's folks very graciously told me, "Tom, we know you need a wife and Tim needs a mother. All we ask is that Pam love him and treat him right."

I didn't know if Tim would call her Mother just because I wanted him to or if it would really meet a need in his heart. My fears were erased on a Sunday morning. We had been at Hemet for the weekend, and when I told Tim it was time to leave for home, he replied, "I'm not going."

With feelings of anger rising within me, I demanded, "What do you mean, you're not going?"

Then, with all the love and tenderness that a three-year-old could muster, he said, "Daddy, I love Mother more than you."

Pam and I stood and wept. We knew the battle had been won; we knew the Lord had wrought a great victory.

Graduation was drawing near, and the wedding date had been set for July. It was time to find a place to begin our married life. As we looked for housing around the Los Angeles area, we met a widow in Alhambra who had made her home into a duplex. That was to be our first home. On weekends, Pam would come up to the home of Wanda's folks and we would go to the duplex on Saturdays and work on decorating it. By the time of the wedding, she had our home ready for the three of us.

As I walked into the barber shop on July 10, 1959, I could hardly believe that I was getting my hair cut for the wedding. The drive down to Hemet seemed like a thousand miles. I was sure that day had more hours in it than any I had ever known!

Pam looked beautiful in her wedding gown, and her olive complexion highlighted the white satin and lace. Her dark eyes glistened from under the veil, and her radiant smile made me forget all the pain I had previously known.

The wedding went very smoothly except for one small interruption, which we look back on with joy. When I walked in and took my place beside the preacher, awaiting the entrance of the bride, Tim (with all the gusto of his little voice) said, "That's my daddy!"

Everyone had a good laugh, and we proceeded with the ceremony.

Pam had graduated; July had finally arrived; and the little seventeen-year-old girl from Hemet had become Mrs. Tom Williams. Tim's and my tomorrows would be so much better.

4   The Young Mother

After our honeymoon, it was almost unbelievable how smoothly Pam assumed her responsibilities as mother. It took Tim a little while to adjust to being away from Grandma, but Pam was very patient, and the two of them soon became inseparable. Both Pam and Tim always had a lot to tell me each day when I came home from work—either that they had been to the zoo, the park or some other place a four-year-old boy liked to go.

Pam was young and looked even younger, and we had a lot of laughs as people stared and wondered how such a young girl could be the mother of this little boy.

As I look back on our situation, other than having given birth to Tim, Pam really was a mother to him in every way, loving him as her very own.

We had been married just a short while when Tim had to have very serious eye surgery. No mother ever stayed closer to a little one's hospital bed than Pam did. And she so diligently cared for his eye during the healing period, making many trips to Long Beach to take Tim to a clinic that specialized in retraining the eye muscles.

When it came time for Tim to start school, no mother could have handled the leaving processes and activities any better than she did.

Our First Child

Just thirteen months after we were married, Pam gave birth

to our first child. Phyllis was a blonde-haired, blue-eyed little girl. Tim was elated with his baby sister. His first reaction was, "Can I play with her?" We explained that it would be a while before she could play, but that he could hug and kiss her. There was never any jealousy in his heart over the new arrival. He just seemed happy to have a baby in the house.

The new baby presented a real challenge to Pam, since she was still working at being all our five-year-old needed in a mother. In order to lighten her load I changed diapers, mopped the floors, cooked some of the meals, made beds and did lots of other things. It meant so much to Pam to have my help.

Just nine months after our little girl was born, the Lord called me to be an evangelist. I quit my job as a salesman for the Coca-Cola Bottling Company of Los Angeles the same day God spoke to my heart. When the Lord started opening doors, I began to travel. Sometimes I was gone for several weeks at a time. At first, Pam wondered if this was really the Lord's leading in our lives. However, it soon became apparent to her that this was what the Lord wanted since His blessings were so evident. Although it was hard for us to be apart and very difficult for her to care for the children alone, Pam never again complained or questioned my decision.

When Phyllis was three years old, the Lord sent us a baby boy. Paul had all of Pam's features—olive-colored skin, dark brown eyes and dark brown hair. Paul became a real delight to us. Tim and Phyllis (and especially Tim) were thrilled to have a little brother.

Paul lacked about two months being four years old when our last child was born. This time the Lord blessed us with a little girl who was the very image of her mother. Penny was and still is like her mother in almost every way.

For eighteen years the little girl from Hemet, California, proved to be the most wonderful wife and mother that a man and his children could know. I have been reminded many times of the words of her pastor, Dr. Ed Rodda. Not long before Pam and I married, he had told me, "Tom, you are getting the finest, most godly young lady I have ever known." He surely was right.

From His throne in Heaven, our Father had chosen earth's best and had given her to me. How I praise and thank Him for the love and joys we shared during those years!

5 | Valley of the Shadow of Death

The grief-filled tomorrow with my second wife began in 1978. We had gone to Israel on a Bible lands tour and had been there for about nine or ten days when tragedy struck. On March 7, as we were riding the tramcar up the steep precipice called Masada, which rises several hundred feet out of the desert floor, Pam suddenly began to tremble and jerk and to have excruciating pain in her lower back. I asked her what was wrong. She didn't know. I asked if she had been sick and had not told me. She said she had not.

When the tramcar reached the landing, I picked her up in my arms and immediately ran up the steps to the top of the mountain. We tried to make her as comfortable as we could, covering her with several coats since she was having chills.

As quickly as possible, we helped her down the other side of the mountain and rushed her by ambulance to Beersheba, Israel, where she was admitted to the hospital. After about seven hours, the doctors told me there was nothing they could do for Pam. They couldn't find what was causing the pain in her lower back, and they didn't feel she had been sick long enough for them to correctly diagnose the problem. Their advice was to get her back to the United States as quickly as possible.

Having no other means of transportation, I called a taxicab. The driver took us the one hundred miles to Tel Aviv, Israel, where we took the next plane back to the States.

Upon our arrival in America, Pam was taken immediately to

the Alexandria Hospital in Alexandria, Virginia, near Washington, D.C.

After an examination, she was admitted to the emergency ward, and the doctor instructed the nurses to begin intravenous feeding. Pam responded to that. The first diagnosis was that she had some kind of virus and probably would be well enough to go home in three or four days. However, the diagnosis was not correct; and later that night she began saying things that had no meaning at all.

We realized that Pam didn't know what she was saying, and the doctor insisted that a psychiatrist check her. I told him her problem was not mental, but physical. But he told me he would not proceed with Pam's case unless I gave permission to call in a psychiatrist. Since she so desperately needed help, I consented.

By the time the psychiatrist arrived, Pam couldn't speak at all; she could communicate only with her eyes or by nodding or shaking her head. After asking her a few questions, the psychiatrist confirmed what I had told the doctor—that Pam's problem was physical. He went on to say that, if the medical doctors did not do something soon, it would be too late.

At that point, an internal specialist, Dr. Shih, told me he would take the case. He immediately asked me to sign papers, giving him permission to perform a lower lumbar puncture on my wife.

Some time later he came back and told me Pam had the worst case of bacterial meningitis he had seen in his entire medical career. The spinal pressure was over 300, and her spinal fluid— which should have looked like tap water—had the consistency of buttermilk. Dr. Shih said Pam had lapsed into a coma after having a grand mal seizure and that she probably had less than twenty-four hours to live.

When I asked if anything could be done medically, he said Pam had the meningococcal variety of meningitis, which was subject to penicillin, but she would require massive doses. He felt it futile to administer the penicillin because he didn't believe she would live.

Although Dr. Shih gave me no hope, I pleaded with him to at least try it. He gave her twenty-four *million* units then, followed by another twenty-four million units three and one-half hours later and a million units every hour for the next fourteen days.

After that time, with still seemingly no hope for Pam, the doctors said that even if she survived, she would be an absolute vegetable for the rest of her very short life.

Dr. Shih and three infectious disease specialists had collaborated on the case during this fourteen-day period, and they were convinced that Pam would be dead in two more days. They moved her from the intensive care unit to the acute care ward, which meant she would be across from the nurses' station. They had heard through the hospital office that I had no health insurance, and they did not want to keep running up the bill, which by then was in the thousands of dollars. The cost for acute care was not as expensive as for intensive care.

The doctors suggested I put Pam in a nursing home, but I just couldn't do that. I pleaded with them to leave her in the hospital. They agreed to keep her, and Pam was there four more weeks, making her stay in the Alexandria Hospital a total of six weeks.

Let me say here that my reason for not having insurance is that God very definitely, at the beginning of mine and Pam's marriage, asked us not to have insurance. He impressed on both of our hearts that we were to live by faith. I am not opposed to others' having health insurance. In fact, I feel that others should have it. I just know that God asked Pam and me to trust Him for our needs.

Since that time, we have been in the hospital several times. Pam, of course, was in the hospital when our children were born, and I was in the hospital in 1968 with a heart problem. Since

God had miraculously paid those bills, we knew He would pay this one.

In fact, the second day Pam was in the Alexandria Hospital, the lady from the financial office asked me to stop by and see her. When I arrived, she began, "We see by the admission papers that you do not have insurance."

"That is true."

"Mr. Williams, this bill is running $1,600 a day; you can see that it soon will add up to a lot of money. How do you hope to pay the bill?"

"By cash."

She queried, "Do you have that kind of cash?"

"No, ma'am."

"Well, where do you expect to get it?"

"From my Father."

"Does your father have that kind of money?"

"Yes, ma'am, He sure does!"

She then asked, "Can you contact him?"

"Yes, ma'am."

"Today?"

"Yes, ma'am."

"Can you contact him by three o'clock today?"

"Yes, I can."

She said, "Well, call your father and tell him we need $3,000 by three o'clock this afternoon!"

"Yes, ma'am, I'll do that."

"You seem so sure that you can reach your father."

I told her, "Yes, I was speaking with Him just before you called me down here, and I know He is in."

Of course, she didn't understand that I was referring to my Heavenly Father.

I went to the elevator and started back up to the intensive care unit. There on the elevator, all alone, I spoke to my Heavenly Father. "Father, this is Tom."

He said, "I know."

"Father, Pam is sick."

He answered, "I know."

I continued: "Father, they want $3,000 by three o'clock this afternoon." He assured me in my heart that He would take care of the need.

As I stepped off the elevator and started down the hall, I was met by Dr. Bud Calvert, pastor of the Fairfax Baptist Temple, a church in the area where I had spoken a number of times. Dr. Calvert said, "Good morning, Tom; how's Pam?"

"Praise the Lord! She's still alive!"

"That's wonderful! Our church prayed for her all night. I just went home this morning to shave and clean up so I could come and be with you."

He then asked, "Where have you been?"

"Down to the financial office."

"What did they want?"

"Three thousand dollars by three o'clock this afternoon!"

He sort of grinned. "That's wonderful! While I was home shaving, some of the men I prayed with all night called and said, 'Pastor, Brother Williams will be needing some money, and we would like you to go by the church treasurer's house and get him a check for $3,500. We'll put it back in the offering on Sunday.'"

Brother Calvert reached into his pocket and pulled out the check. Across the bottom was written, "We just want you to know that we love you."

God alone knows how much Pastor Bud Calvert means to me. I already considered him my friend, but as he stayed by me so faithfully during our vigil, I grew to love him very dearly and to appreciate him so very much.

After Brother Calvert handed me the check, I got back on

the elevator and went down to the financial office. In less than ten minutes from the time the lady told me she needed $3,000, God had supplied not only the money she requested, but an additional $500!

Greatly surprised when I handed her the check, she exclaimed, "That's remarkable!"

I replied, "Yes, it is!"

Two days later, she told me they needed another $4,000. I told her, "Yes, ma'am. I'll contact my Father," which I did in the elevator going back up to Pam's room.

Just as I stepped off the elevator and started down the hall, the telephone rang at the nurses' station. Since no one was at the desk, I answered the phone. The calls had been for us most of the time anyway. In fact, we had been getting so many calls that they had assigned a special operator at the hospital just to take our calls.

When I answered the phone, I recognized the voice of my pastor from Denver, Colorado—Dr. Ed Nelson—on the other end of the line.

With noticeable concern in his voice, he asked, "Tom, how is Pam?"

I replied, "Still alive, Pastor."

"That's tremendous! We are really praying for her." (They did pray at South Sheridan Baptist Church! And how I appreciate them and the efforts they put forth on our behalf in prayer and help!)

He then asked, "Tom, how are the finances?"

"Well, I just came from the office downstairs, and they need $4,000."

Pastor Nelson said, "Praise the Lord! We took an offering for you last night, and it was $4,120. You can get a check from Brother Calvert, and we will send him this one."

Later that day, I got the check from Dr. Calvert and took it to the financial office, still in awe at God's goodness. When I handed the check to the lady, she said, "That's remarkable!"

I said, "Yes, it really is!"

Let me say here: Isn't it wonderful, my friend, that God *does* know our needs! He is a *personal* God. We are not just a number in His computer. I am so thankful for that!

God again met our need when we were making plans to have Pam transferred from Alexandria Hospital to Mercy Hospital in Denver, Colorado, where we were living at that time.

Pam had been in the hospital for six weeks and had not made any apparent progress. I felt we needed to return to Denver so the children could start back to school, since Pam was no longer able to teach them at home.

The doctors told us that Pam would have to be transported by a jet airplane. We checked into the possibility of using a commercial airline, but with all the restrictions involved in transporting a comatose patient—renting a section of the plane and curtaining it off from the other passengers, hiring two registered nurses to travel with us, and various other problems—it just didn't seem this was the answer. I checked with a private agency, but they wanted $7,000 for the flight. This did not seem feasible either.

Finally, the Lord reminded me that a friend, Jerry Smith, had a jet plane. I tried calling Jerry, but he was not in his office. I called his folks, but they didn't have the number where he was staying. "Tom, he is in Hawaii on an extended vacation and doesn't want to be bothered."

I thanked them, then dropped to my knees there in the waiting room of the hospital and prayed, "Father, You know where Jerry is; please have him call me. I sure do need that plane."

Not more than five minutes had passed when the telephone rang in the hospital waiting room. I answered it, and the operator said, "Please hold for Jerry Smith; Maui, Hawaii."

My, what a great God we have! We cannot ask things that He cannot do!

Jerry said, "Tom, I was walking along the beach not more than five minutes ago when I felt an unusual urgency to call you. What do you need?"

I jubilantly replied, "Jerry, just about five minutes ago I prayed that God would have you call me!" Then I explained our dilemma. "I know this is asking a big favor, and I know it costs a lot of money to fly a Lear jet; but Jerry, I sure need that plane."

He kindly told me, "Tom, just tell me when and where you need the plane, and it will be there."

My! Isn't God wonderful! Thank the Lord for Jerry and Mrs. Smith and their generosity!

Beginning of a Long Journey

Jerry's pilots went by the Denver airport and picked up Dr. Ralph Roland, our family physician, and took him to Washington, D.C. I met Dr. Roland at the airport and drove him to the Alexandria Hospital. Dr. Roland spent three hours going over Pam's records and discussing them with Dr. Shih. In the meantime, I went down to the office to settle up financially.

The lady in the finance office said, "Mr. Williams, I just want you to know that I have never seen anything like this, and neither has this hospital. So much money has come in for your wife's bill that we owe you a refund. It will take us about a week to process everything through the computer. Can you trust us for it?"

I almost told her, "No, I need it by four o'clock!" But I said, "That will be fine."

She said, "I think you should know that Dr. Shih's bill has not been turned in."

I thanked her and went back upstairs. Dr. Shih had released Pam into Dr. Roland's care, and she was on a stretcher being rolled toward the ambulance that was to take us to the plane.

Walking down the hallway of the hospital, Dr. Shih put his arm around me in obvious concern. I said, "Dr. Shih, I just settled the bill with the finance office downstairs, and the lady there said you have not yet submitted a bill. I can give you $3,000 this morning and will be happy to pay the balance at $100 a week if that is suitable to you. I promise to be faithful."

Dr. Shih was not a man who knew Jesus Christ, but he looked up at me and said, "Mr. Williams, there is no bill. I just wish I had your faith"—and he simply wrote off the entire amount!

I don't know how much his bill would have been, but I do know that the Bible says, "The king's heart is in the hand of the Lord, as the rivers of water: he turneth it whithersoever he will" (Prov. 21:1). God had again intervened for us in a tremendous way.

We flew to Denver. Pam was admitted to the Mercy Hospital where Dr. Roland had assembled a team of neurosurgeons and neurologists. For two weeks they went over every part of her body, doing everything that medical science taught—EEGs, cat scans, spinal taps and other things, including arteriograph tests, where they inserted an instrument in the artery of the leg and channeled it to the heart, the neck and into the brain, checking for any clue that would help them know how to treat her.

After their examination, they concluded that Pam was indeed a total vegetable and that she would never be any different than she was right then.

Since the specialists did not feel they could help Pam, I talked to Dr. Roland, a wonderful Christian, and persuaded him to let me take Pam home and care for her. Even though we lived in a motor home because of our traveling to and from meetings, I felt she would do better in a family atmosphere of love than she would at the hospital.

The nurses worked with me at the hospital for three days,

teaching me how to feed Pam through the tube in her stomach, run the catheter, take her blood pressure and do other things for her.

When I brought Pam home the last of April, 1978, she weighed only eighty-nine pounds. Her little body was twisted and deformed. Her toes had rolled back under her feet; her feet had turned straight down; her legs had rolled in toward each other; her left hand had closed and turned back up her left arm; her right hand was open and would not close; all of her fingers were gnarled and totally deformed; her eyes were locked; her neck was set; and her mouth was pulled to one side like that of a stroke victim. In that condition I began to take care of her.

I kept the same kind of records that the nurses kept when Pam was in the hospital. Dr. Roland came to our home twice a week to check the records and take blood samples. (I was told that the only way doctors can tell if a comatose person is healthy is through blood tests.)

Two young therapists who had taken an interest in Pam's case volunteered to come to the house once a week to teach me therapy. I worked with Pam during the week, administering the therapy they taught me, and I learned additional techniques each week when they came.

Eight or nine hours a day were spent trying to straighten Pam's limbs. Although she was in a coma and couldn't speak, we could tell by the expressions on her face that the therapy was excruciatingly painful. But we knew that if we did not continue, her body would never be normal. I just kept working with her, even though doctors offered no hope at all that my efforts would bring results.

Four months passed; Pam was still in the coma. By this time God had put a burning desire in my heart to start back preaching. Even though well-meaning friends had told us it was impossible for Pam to travel in her condition, I knew that I had to obey the Lord.

The children took care of their mother while I drove the motor home to the meetings. Once we got to the church where I would be preaching, I continued working with her during the day and the children took care of her at night while I preached.

Then one night, almost six months after the onset of Pam's illness, God miraculously woke her up. Without my knowing it, my children had covenanted together to pray that their mother would wake up on my birthday, August 17. Pam came out of the coma about 9:30 p.m. on August 18.

The children did not tell me about their prayers concerning Pam until after she woke up. Although God did not answer their prayer on my birthday, they did not despair. They prayed on August 18 just like they had prayed the previous days and weeks. They believed Jeremiah 33:3: "Call unto me, and I will answer thee."

That night started out like so many other nights. I was preaching in Knoxville, Tennessee, and the children were staying with their mother in the motor home, parked in the parking lot of the church.

After I returned to the motor home, the children and I had some refreshments and were preparing for bed. Because of the crowded condition of the motor home, the children would individually come to our room and tell us goodnight.

Some weeks earlier, our youngest son Paul had given his mother a small, multi-colored stuffed dog. Because of the various colors in the fabric, we had named the dog Rainbow. Each night when Paul came to tell us goodnight, he would bring Rainbow. Holding it in front of his mother, he would say, "Mom, this is Rainbow." Then he would ask her, "What is his name?"

Of course, Pam didn't answer. But Paul continued to bring the dog night after night, saying the same words each time. Lovingly, he would place Rainbow in the bed beside Pam and say, "Rainbow is going to sleep with you." Then each morning as he came to tell us good morning, he would get Rainbow and put him up until the next evening.

On August 18, Paul took Rainbow to his mother and, as he had done so many times in the past, said, "Mom, this is Rainbow. What is his name?" Just as he started to leave the room, Pam opened her eyes and, for the first time in almost six months, answered us. Very slowly she said, "R-r-rainbow."

Paul and I looked at each other, hardly believing what we had heard. Then we shouted, "Mommy is awake!" And the other children came running into the room.

Weeping so much, we could hardly talk! In a few minutes, I looked into Pam's face and said, "This is Tom." She stared at me for a few seconds and then mumbled, "Tom."

Heartbroken, I realized that Pam did not recognize us or understand anything we said; she merely was repeating what she had heard.

I ran to the telephone and called Dr. Roland in Denver, Colorado. I told him step by step what had happened, and he confirmed what I had suspected: "Pam will have to learn everything all over again."

Dr. Roland suggested that I begin by teaching her to crawl. I purchased some silk sheets, as I felt this type fabric would make it easier for her to move about as we taught her to crawl. One of the ladies of the church graciously offered to sew them together.

During the day, at the various churches where I was holding meetings, I would spread the sheets in a large area and take Pam in my arms and place her on her stomach. Since her body was deformed and her muscles were spastic from having been in a coma for so long, she suffered excruciating pain when I put her on the floor. She would scream and cry; she would scratch us and spit on us, trying to get us to leave her alone. But I knew that in order to help her, we had to hurt her. I thank God that He gave us the grace to keep doing what we had to do.

The children would push back on her shoulders as I pushed one leg and then the other, moving them forward in a crawling motion. We spent hundreds of hours, but it was worth it when she finally crawled.

Then we had to teach Pam to sit, stand, feed herself, tie her shoes and brush her teeth. We taught her how to say the ABCs, to count, to recognize colors and many other things—just like we would teach a young child.

We have spent literally thousands of hours on various kinds of therapy we learned from books and therapists. We have walked Pam more than 3,300 miles, trying to teach her to walk correctly again. She does walk, but with a robot-type shuffle.

It took me fourteen months to toilet train her. I diapered Pam just like I would diaper a baby. I trained her by tying her on a commode for long periods at a time. I was told she could never be toilet trained, but, praise the Lord, she was! Pam can take herself to the bathroom now, but we still have to clean her afterward.

It has been several years since Pam became ill. She has made much progress, but there are many things she still cannot do for herself. She cannot do her hair, bathe, dress herself or do any kind of housework. The children and I did all of this for three years. Finally, as the children began marrying and leaving home, I came to the realization that I had to hire someone to help take care of Pam. For the past few years, we have had a nurse living and traveling with us.

Pam looks to me for total security. We have a relationship somewhat like a father and daughter. For this reason, she goes almost everywhere I go. We fly about 100,000 miles a year as I tell our story and preach the old, old story of the Gospel of

our Lord Jesus Christ. We have seen thousands come to a personal knowledge of Jesus Christ as their Saviour, and hundreds
of thousands of lives have been changed in other ways.

We have seen divorced couples remarry. Couples who were
separated have gotten back together. And folks who thought
they could not get along with each other now have a sweet marriage. Many have learned not to complain about their situation,
but instead, to be thankful.

I will tell you in a later chapter about the wonderful film the
Lord has enabled us to produce for His glory concerning this
story. But for now, let me say, "To God be the glory. Great
things He has done!"

6   **Hope in the Midst of Despair**

At the time Pam became ill, our family was living in a motor home. The Tom Williams Evangelistic Ministries had purchased some Continental Silver Eagle buses and had them converted into motor homes. We had three to accommodate the families who traveled in our evangelistic team.

Several months into our trial I realized I had to make a decision: either put Pam in a rehabilitation center or nursing home so I could be free to pursue my evangelistic work or disband the team and let each family find another area of ministry.

The blessed Holy Spirit began to speak to me from Ephesians 5:25. The words, "Husbands, love your wives, even as Christ also loved the church, and gave himself for it," began to burn their way into my heart. I knew beyond a shadow of doubt that my highest calling was to be the husband God wanted me to be.

The Lord opened doors of service for the other members of the team, and we started trying to sell the motor homes. When we traveled, diesel fuel (which was what the buses used) was much less expensive than gasoline. This was one of the big selling points for the buses. But just as we put them up for sale, the price of diesel fuel was raised to about the same price as gasoline, causing prospective buyers to reconsider.

We finally sold two of the motor homes, but we took a real loss on them. Since we were unable to clear the debt against them, the last one (the one we were living in) was repossessed by the bank on January 1, 1980.

We had received a two-week notice and during that time had asked the Lord to give us a place to live. God put it on the heart of a man in Texas to call and say he would send $500 a month to help us rent a home. I was able to find a nice place for $495 a month.

Having lived in a motor home for the last five years, we had no furniture except one chair. So we moved into a three-bedroom home with one chair, five sleeping bags, dishes and cooking utensils. A built-in stove came with the house.

I spent many hours in prayer about our situation. Some of the folks in our home church gave us a bed, a dresser and a dining room table with chairs.

The Lord kept bringing to my mind a man named Melvin Layne, who lived on the other side of Denver from us. I knew him but had not seen him in years. When I called Mel and asked if I could come and talk with him, he very kindly said I could.

I drove across town, praying all the while that the Lord would burden his heart for our needs. After exchanging greetings, Mel and his wife invited me to sit down. As I told them about Pam's condition and our dire financial circumstances, my spirit was so broken that I wept. When I finished, he looked at me and said, "Tom, I'm glad God sent you to our home."

I knew then that God had answered my prayer.

Mel and his wife asked me to walk with them through their house. He pointed out several pieces of furniture and said, "You can have this." From their own home, they gave us enough to finish furnishing the various rooms of our house except for the master bedroom and some appliances. Then Mel turned to me and said, "Tom, you meet us at Levitz' Furniture Company tomorrow morning."

The next day the three of us walked into the furniture store and began to look around. Mel asked, "What would Pam choose if she were able?"

Very hesitatingly, I told him she was partial to Mediterranean.

He replied, "Good! That's what she is going to have."

We went to the bedroom furniture department, and he and his wife began putting together the most beautiful bedroom suite I had ever seen. They selected a three-post king-size bed, double-mirror dresser, five-drawer chest, two night stands and matching lamps. Then he said to the salesman, "I also want your most expensive mattress set."

After Mel had made these purchases, he looked at me and said, "Now for the appliances!" He called Sears and asked them to deliver a washer, dryer and a refrigerator-freezer to our home and send him the bill.

His wife Charlene asked me when we would be gone for a couple of days. I told her, and she asked, "May I have a key to your house?"

When we returned from our trip, I could hardly believe my eyes. She had put new drapes where they were needed. She also had put a beautiful king-size bedspread and matching throw pillows on our bed and had put bedspreads on the children's beds to match their drapes.

Their generosity again overwhelmed me. It was like a dream, too good to be true, but it was true.

That happened several years ago, but I still weep when I think of the love shown to us by Mr. and Mrs. Melvin Layne. All I can say is, "Thank You, Heavenly Father, and thank you, Mel and Charlene!"

God had again met a need in our lives when, humanly speaking, we were facing an impossible situation. How thankful I am that God is not limited by our own financial resources! He has ways of supplying our needs and doing "exceeding abundantly above all that we ask or think, according to the power that worketh in us" (Eph. 3:20).

7 Breaking Up the Nest

By the middle of 1981, which was just over three years after Pam first became ill, her condition was about the same as it had been after two years, except her ability to make conversation had improved. She still required total care.

Although Pam's situation was about the same, my situation was changing drastically as the children began to leave the nest.

Tim (our oldest son) had married while Pam was in the coma. Some time later Phyllis had become reacquainted with a young man she had known in her childhood. His name was Paul Williams (the same name as our younger son). Paul had met a real need in Phyllis's heart and life.

Phyllis had been doing most of the cooking and cleaning and had so wonderfully stepped in and helped take care of her mother and the younger children. She felt a deep sense of responsibility to stay home and help us, yet she dearly loved Paul and had a very natural desire for a home of her own. And even though I knew that her getting married would leave a tremendous empty spot in our home, I felt she should tell Paul she would marry him.

What Now?

Not knowing how I would manage when Phyllis left, I again went to my Heavenly Father in prayer and asked Him to show me what I was supposed to do.

Our finances were already so strained that it seemed we just couldn't take on the additional expenses of hiring someone to help. Since we no longer had the motor home, we were flying to our meetings. I was taking Phyllis and Pam with me and paying someone to live at our home and take care of Paul and Penny so they could continue their schooling. (Phyllis had already graduated.)

One day Paul and Penny came to me in tears and said, "Daddy, we cannot go on this way. We no longer have a mother, and our daddy is gone all the time. We *need* you."

Because of this, I had dropped back to having one meeting a month so I could spend more time at home, and that just was not sufficient to pay the bills. We had cut back to the bare necessities and were no longer buying things like orange juice, potato chips and so many other things that the children would have enjoyed: now to think of trying to hire someone full-time to help with Pam seemed like an impossibility.

But the Lord seemed to give peace that the need would be met financially and that I should go ahead and look for someone to help us.

As I continued to pray for someone to replace Phyllis, God kept bringing to mind a young lady named Janice Williams, the sister of Phyllis's fiancé, Paul. Even though we had the same last name, Janice was not related to us.

Janice worked at a day-care center for a church in Kansas City, Missouri. What I did not know was that God also was speaking to Janice's heart about our needs.

It is always interesting to see how our Heavenly Father will work out the details in bringing people into our lives and meeting our needs. Earlier in 1981, when it seemed I had reached the end of my resources emotionally, I was on my knees in the bedroom, weeping and crying out to God, "Father, I just need to hear from You in a real special way right now—in a way that would let me know You are saying 'Amen' to all we are doing and going through," when the telephone rang.

I picked up the phone and was surprised to hear the voice of Dr. A. A. Baker who, at that time, was Vice-President of Pensacola Christian College in Pensacola, Florida—a wonderful Christian training center for young people. He said, "Brother Williams, I am calling on behalf of our President, Dr. A. R. Horton. If you would accept it, we would like to give you an honorary doctorate at graduation this year." I said to Dr. Baker, "You will never know how much this telephone call means to me."

It was such a tremendous encouragement that they would want to honor me in this way. But I saw their willingness to honor me with a doctorate as God's "Amen," saying, "I am watching, Son, and I care. Here is just a bit of encouragement to help you face tomorrow."

I'm so thankful that God is so personal and knows each of our needs and, yes, each of our heartaches. He loves and cares beyond description. His mercies are new every morning, and His compassions never fail (Lam. 3:22,23).

When it came time to go to Pensacola Christian College to receive my doctorate, we drove a van down to Pensacola, Florida, because I wanted to take a number of people with me, including my wife, some of my children and my secretary who had been so faithful in the office in Denver—so they could see me honored in this way.

On the way to Pensacola, I felt impressed to call Janice right away. So I stopped at a service station, walked over to the pay phone and called her in Kansas City. I said, "Janice, I have been praying about something, and I want to talk to you about it. What I'm about to say may not interest you at all. I will tell you in a moment what I can pay and what your responsibilities would be."

Janice interrupted me. "Mr. Williams, you don't need to go any further. The Spirit of God has been speaking to my heart, and I know you are calling about my coming to live with your family and take care of Mrs. Williams. I need to give a two-week notice at the day care. Then I will be there because I know that is the will of God for my life."

Again, my Heavenly Father had so wonderfully met our need, and we knew beyond doubt that Janice was the person for the job.

Janice came about a week before Phyllis's wedding, so Phyllis could explain her responsibilities concerning the cooking and housework and teach her how to take care of Pam. So by the time our fledgling left the nest on May 29, God had provided a helper to take her place.

Heart-rending Loneliness

When Phyllis married, it was so much different than when Tim married. Since Pam was incapable of helping Phyllis in the ways a mother ordinarily would help, I had to plan the wedding. I went to the bridal shop to help Phyllis pick out her dress. I also designed the cake and tried to fill in everywhere I could.

I remember so vividly performing the ceremony that night with a lot of tears. But the tears *really* flowed when I returned home and found Phyllis's good-bye note on my pillow, thanking me for all the things I had done for her and for stepping in and doing the things her mother would have done had she been able.

That was a heart-rending experience, and I wept into the wee hours of the morning, with no one to talk to but the Lord. Please don't misunderstand; it was precious talking to Him, but I longed to turn to my dear wife and discuss all the joys of the wedding, the guests, plans for the future and other things which couples ordinarily discuss after returning from the wedding of their daughter.

But not to be able to turn to my wife and share these precious moments with her was especially hard for me. She had been a wonderful friend and companion before her illness; now Pam showed no emotion about anything. She really did not comprehend what was involved in Phyllis's getting married and leaving home.

So instead of turning to Pam, I turned to the Lord for His grace to strengthen and help me to face tomorrow.

Another Fledgling Leaves the Nest

Just a few days before Phyllis's wedding, our youngest son Paul had graduated from high school. I tried to spend as much time with him that summer as possible because I knew, from the experience of having seen our two older children go off to college, that things are never quite the same once young people reach this stage in life. Even though they may come home for Christmas and during the summer, they have reached a real milestone in their lives as they begin to mature toward adulthood and start thinking of their future and a home of their own.

So the nest was breaking up even further. In September, 1981, Paul left for Pensacola Christian College. This left me with Penny and with Janice, the young lady who had come to help take care of my wife.

A real sense of loneliness began to crowd into my heart as I realized the children were leaving and that it would not be very long—just four more years—until the nest would be completely empty. But I had daughter Penny to hold onto and to help ease my loneliness during this time.

Since Penny looked so much like her mother had looked at her age, and since she was like Pam in almost every way, Penny was a tremendous joy to me. I began to lose myself in doing for her and seeing my wife really come alive again in Penny. Knowing that she would one day be married, I tried to teach her to be the young lady God wanted her to be, the wife and mother she eventually would be and what Pam would have taught her to be had she been able.

In addition to spending time with Penny and teaching her the things she needed to know, my heart was ever entwined in my dear wife's life, trying to be what I needed to be to her and instilling in her the security of always having me close at hand. By this time she was traveling with me everywhere, even though she still required constant care. Penny did her schooling through a correspondence course so she could travel with us. The four of us, including the nurse, began to fly to all our meetings, spending as much time together as we possibly could.

When we were home, our daughter would help with the cooking, the laundry and many other things. On the nurse's day off, Penny would take her place. That put a tremendous responsibility on such a young girl and made her mature more quickly than she should have or would have under normal circumstances.

Realizing how quickly our daughter was growing up and knowing that she, too, would be leaving home in a few years, I tried to make every moment count. One day I asked Penny, "If I were to buy a large motorcycle, would you be interested in just the two of us getting away for a couple of weeks' vacation each summer for the next three years, seeing some of the country and just being together and having a wonderful time as father and daughter?" She thought that a tremendous idea.

The first summer after I purchased the motorcycle, we went to Cody, Wyoming. We saw some beautiful sites, spent some time at The King's Ranch (a Christian home for homeless children), and visited with our friends, the Wells family. Then we traveled back across some of the mountains of Wyoming, down into the Black Hills of South Dakota, seeing Mount

Rushmore and visiting many other sites on our way back to Denver, Colorado.

God was so good to give us that time together, and I'm so glad that our all-wise Heavenly Father does not allow us to know all the details of the future. Little did I know that would be the only summer we would be able to vacation together in this way, for the very next summer Penny met Todd Lehigh, the young man she was to marry.

It was almost ironic to see so many parallels in Todd and Penny's lives as compared to Pam's and mine. Pam and I had met when she was sixteen and I was twenty-three; we had married when Pam was seventeen. When Penny met Todd, he was twenty-three and she was sixteen.

As a rule, I had allowed my children to date only about four times during their high school career, feeling they should have a lot of companionship with other young people. So when Penny met Todd, at first I only allowed him to write to her.

Todd was such a gentleman about doing exactly what I asked on behalf of my daughter. As I saw the maturity in Penny's life and his, and as I recalled what a capable wife and mother to my four-year-old son Pam had been at seventeen, and how much Penny was like Pam in so many ways, I broke some rules I had established and enforced with the other children. I could have enforced the rules, but it did not seem wise to do so because of the situations that had developed in our home with Pam's illness and Penny's having to do the work of a woman.

So Todd began coming to see Penny. I did not let him take her out at first. They dated by doing things with us. Their relationship grew in a wonderful and godly way. Todd loved the Lord and was serving Him. Since he already had his college degree and was financially capable of providing for a wife, I consented to their getting married the following summer.

Penny and Todd set a wedding date for July 14, 1984. They

wanted very much to get married on our twenty-fifth wedding anniversary, which was July 10, but that was on a Tuesday and Todd could not take off work in the middle of the week to get married and still have a week for their honeymoon. So they decided to get married on July 14.

Penny wore the same wedding dress her mother had worn twenty-five years earlier. It looked like it had been tailor-made for her. The people who had seen Pam in her wedding dress at seventeen said it was as though she had discovered the fountain of youth and was again seventeen years old.

As I looked at my lovely daughter in her mother's wedding dress, tears coursed down my cheeks as my mind was flooded with memories of the many wonderful times Pam and I had shared during those early days, long before her illness.

Todd and Penny were married in our backyard. The ferns waved softly in the gentle breeze of the beautiful July day. All eyes were fastened on the lovely young bride as she made her way ever so sweetly toward her waiting bridegroom.

Our other children all came for the wedding, and Terry (Tim's wife) sang a beautiful song to fit the occasion.

Dr. Wendell Kempton, president of the Association of Baptists for World Evangelism, flew in and participated in the ceremony, along with Dr. Bob Kelley, pastor of the Franklin Road Baptist Church in Murfreesboro, Tennessee, where we had moved in November, 1983.

We were so thankful for all the fine people who attended. Mrs. John R. Rice (widow of the famous preacher and author) was there, along with many friends we had met after moving to Tennessee a few months earlier. Folks came from Iowa, Illinois, New Jersey and various other places to be an encouragement to this young girl who had so wonderfully stood by and cared for her mother. Many paid respect to her for that. Our guests said it was the loveliest wedding they had ever seen.

God again showed His goodness in making it possible for Todd and Penny to go to Hawaii for their honeymoon. Some of my friends from the Uniland Corporation of Puyallup, Washington, had a condominium in Hawaii, and I had won two free trips to Hawaii by flying so much, so we were able to present to them a complete honeymoon package. I felt that God was honoring Penny in this way.

When we told them about the wedding gift, I said to her that the Lord was blessing her because as a little ten-year-old girl, when her mother had been laid aside for His glory, she had so graciously accepted the illness and had been faithful to help take care of her mother. Now God was giving this young couple a honeymoon that so many thousands desire but are unable to have.

Todd and Penny had a precious time together, and their marriage today is sweet and wonderful. I thank God from the depths of my heart for His goodness and mercy.

During the time all these things were taking place in Penny's life, Paul had moved from Pensacola Christian College up to Maranatha Baptist College in Wisconsin. In the fall of 1983, he met the young lady he was to marry, Jeanne Ohler from Pasco, Washington. Their romance was beginning to blossom. Then not far into the second semester it became evident that they were in love. The following summer Paul moved up to Pasco to work, and in August, 1984, Pam and I went to Washington, where I performed the wedding ceremony for Paul and Jeanne.

The trip to Washington was another blessing from our loving Heavenly Father. Through the generosity of Mr. and Mrs. Carl Epperson, all of our children were able to fly to Pasco for the wedding.

I am so grateful that God enabled us—by His grace and through the love and kindness of friends He had touched to help us—to do something special for each of our children when they got married. Surely I'll never be able to praise Him enough for that.

After Penny and then Paul married, the nest was completely empty. When we returned home, a deep sense of loneliness set in as I once again thought of the things Pam and I had discussed before her illness. We had planned, after our children were all married, to have a long second honeymoon. We had never allowed our busy schedules to keep us apart to the point that we felt like strangers, as some couples do when their children are growing up. We very much enjoyed each other's presence and looked forward to spending time alone together, going to visit the children and grandchildren, traveling and enjoying serving the Lord together full-time.

But God has so wonderfully given me the grace to go on for Him and to victoriously face tomorrow. And, as I so often have told folks, what I do not have in my dear wife, I have in the Lord Jesus Christ.

I cannot say that I am not lonely; I cannot say that I do not weep; but I *can* say that the love God gives is the kind that lasts right on through the trials and storms of life—regardless of how great they may be.

8   Love Found a Way

In addition to the adjustments we had to make because our children were marrying and leaving the nest, other pressures also were weighing heavily on my heart.

About four years after the onset of Pam's illness, I began to get a lot of criticism from outside sources concerning my decision to keep her at home and work with her. People were saying I had not done right by Pam and, if I had put her in a nursing home, particularly in a rehabilitation center, she would have made much better progress.

As I said earlier, Pam was talking quite well by this time and was walking, but still with a robot-type shuffle. I had worked hard with her over the months and years, trying to teach her to walk normally. Even though we had walked her many hundreds of miles and had spent literally thousands of hours on therapy of every kind, she just could not learn to walk properly.

We had succeeded in teaching Pam to feed herself, to tie her shoes and to do small things, such as brush her teeth and put on her lipstick. I had taught her the ABCs and, among other things, the major cities of America and of the world and the states and countries where these major cities are located. I felt it might help her as we traveled to know where she was and perhaps be able to better relate to certain areas.

We have not taught her to write again. We tried, but it was so frustrating to her. Some of the therapists told me not to worry about the things that were not *really* necessary to living and her enjoyment of life. So we majored only on the things that would make life enjoyable for her.

We taught her to read again, and this helps pass the time for her as we travel. She enjoys reading the road signs and identifying certain makes of cars. She knows almost all the various kinds of cars—either by their grill, insignia or other distinguishing mark. She amazes the people she rides with as she identifies cars, saying, "That's a Mercedes...that's a Cadillac...that's a Chevrolet...that's a Ford...and so forth"—sometimes even before they can tell what kind of car it is.

I sincerely felt I had given my all to help Pam become all that she could be in her mental and physical condition, and we could see such a marked improvement in her. But, of course, when someone compared her to a healthy, normal adult, they naturally could see areas that needed much more improvement.

Finally two businessmen came and offered to pay the bill if I would take Pam to a rehabilitation center to see what her condition really was and to find out whether or not professional therapists felt they could do more for her than I was doing. Another man offered to send us to Mayo Clinic. I knew that was not what Pam needed; but I finally agreed to take her to Craig Rehabilitation Center in Denver, said to be one of the top three such centers in the world.

Their schedule was so heavy that we had to wait four months to get an appointment for Pam to see Dr. Cilo, who reportedly is one of the best neurosurgeons anywhere in America.

Dr. Cilo interviewed my wife in the presence of a number of therapists from various fields—physical, occupational and speech. Each of them looked at Pam. After about an hour of questioning her, examining all her joints and having her do a number of exercises, Dr. Cilo asked, "Mr. Williams, you did all of your wife's therapy?"

"Yes, by the grace of God, I did," was my answer.

He knew what her body had looked like before I started working with her, since I had explained all that to him during the interview. Then this great therapist said, "This is wonderful! I can hardly believe what I am seeing."

I replied, "Dr. Cilo, you *know* that God did it."

He looked at me and very kindly said, "Sir, God has to have hands; and your hands have done a marvelous job. I cannot find a joint in her body that is not absolutely perfect. Not a therapist in the world could have done what you have done. Of course, I hasten to say that what we do here at the Center, we do in concern, care and with all the feeling we can. But what you do, you do with love, and nothing in the world can do what love will do."

At that point, I said, "Dr. Cilo, some of the finest therapists in the country—from the Rockefeller Center on down—have told me that by the time Mrs. Williams was three years into her illness, she would not progress any further. Now here we are four and one-half years later, and she is still improving."

He said, "Craig is one of the finest rehabilitation centers anywhere, and I am supposed to know as much, I suppose, as the next fellow does. But I do not have any way of knowing when your wife will stop learning. I would say that what the therapists said probably would be true under ordinary circumstances, but the way you help your wife and keep working with her, I see no reason why she cannot continue to improve until she dies; and only God knows when that will be."

I asked him, "If Pam were to be admitted to the Craig Rehabilitation Center, could your people really improve on what I am doing?"

He answered, "I could tell you we could. I could treat her as an outpatient, take $2,000 a month from you and work with her for four hours a day. But again I say, What you do, you do with love, and that cannot be improved on."

At that point he walked to his filing cabinet and removed a file folder. "I want you to see something." He handed me a story of a young man who had gone into a coma after being in an automobile accident. He had been admitted to Craig Rehabilitation Center as a comatose patient, since the accident had left him totally paralyzed. He remained in a coma the entire time he was at Craig.

For eleven months he was under the care of some of the finest doctors, therapists and nurses in the world; yet, the only part of his body he could move on command was his right index finger. His body jerked in other places, but he could not so much as blink or move his eyes on command; he could not speak even one word. He could do nothing at all except wiggle that one finger.

The young man's parents lived in Anchorage, Alaska, and they flew down to Denver to visit him. When they realized that their son was making so little progress, they told the doctor they would like to take him home.

As they arrived back in Alaska and rolled the stretcher off the airplane, his brother (who had not seen him since he had become comatose eleven months earlier) met them. As he walked up to the stretcher, he fell on his knees and put his arms around the young man's neck. With tears flowing down his face, he called his comatose brother by name and said, "I love you."

The boy on the stretcher reached up, put his arms around his brother's neck and said, "I love you, too."

After letting me read that story, Dr. Cilo looked at me and said, "Sir, in one minute love did what eleven months of the finest therapy in the world could not do. Go and tell your critics this story."

I'm sure those critical of me probably were sincere, thinking surely there must be something else we could do to help Pam. But I just could not bring myself to put her in a rehabilitation center, a nursing home or any other such place. I knew that what she needed more than anything else was love, constant love.

9   A Break in the Clouds

The Bible says that God never leaves us nor forsakes us. And what a wonderful, blessed promise that is! How many times I have leaned on the great arms of my Heavenly Father and my wonderful Saviour! And the blessed Holy Spirit is such a Comforter as He walks with us through our trials.

God did not say we would not have trials; but the wonderful thing He *did* say was that He would not forsake us. Certainly I can testify to that after these many years of trials.

God wonderfully reminded me of this great truth in January, 1983 while I was in the kitchen getting ready to prepare the evening meal. Again, I had reached a point in my life where I seemingly was at the bottom of the barrel emotionally.

While I worked in the kitchen, tears coursed down my face as I talked to my Father in Heaven. "Lord, this is another of those times when I need something special from You to reassure me that You are still saying 'Amen!' to all I am going through and in the way I'm trying to serve You."

At that precise moment, the telephone rang; it was Dr. Jack Hyles' secretary, Mrs. Erma McKinney. "Brother Williams, Dr. Hyles would like for you to come to Pastors' School in March this year and give your testimony that you told at Hyles-Anderson College last fall."

Dr. Hyles had not personally heard our story, but some of the men in his church, including one of his closest friends, Dr. Russell Anderson, had heard it and had suggested to Dr. Hyles

that he hear it. Feeling that our story would be an encouragement to the pastors, Dr. Hyles invited me to share it at Pastors'
School.

Dr. Jack Hyles is pastor of the First Baptist Church in Hammond, Indiana. He not only pastors one of the largest churches in the world, but he also has the largest Sunday school in
America, averaging around 20,000 each Sunday. The church
has many ministries, one of them being the great Pastors' School.
Every year thousands of pastors gather from all fifty states and
many foreign countries for special in-depth training and encouragement from Dr. Hyles and others he brings in to speak.

When I hung up the phone from talking with Mrs. McKinney, I was so thrilled that my Heavenly Father had again
opened up the clouds and had looked down and said, "Son,
I'm still here, and I'm still in control. I'll help you face tomorrow. And, yes, I'm still using the story to glorify Myself."

As the time drew near for us to go to Pastors' School, I realized
that I would be standing before more people, and especially
pastors, than I had ever stood before at any one gathering. That
was such a momentous occasion in our lives, and I felt very
deeply that my oldest son Tim, who is a pastor, should be there.

Dr. Hyles had made it a practice to show special honor to
the various speakers at Pastors' School, and I wanted Tim to
see firsthand that God rewards those who remain faithful to Him
and continue to serve Him, regardless of circumstances.

So I called him and said, "Tim, I would like for you to be
at Pastors' School when I share the story of our testimony. I
don't have any money, but if you would like to come, I'll send
you an airline ticket and just believe that God will send in the
money to pay for it by the end of the month."

Dr. Hyles had sent money for airline tickets for my wife, myself
and the nurse. We joined Tim at the Chicago airport, where

we were met by Mr. John Olson, one of Dr. Hyles' personal assistants whom I have come to love very much.

Mr. Olson drove us to the hotel, where Dr. Hyles had reserved a room for us. We were treated like kings and queens and were amazed at all the things he had waiting for us—beautiful flowers, a fruit basket, candy, spending money, our meals and hotel accommodations, personal transportation to and from the church, even several quarters in case we got hungry and wanted something from the vending machine! He also had a nice honorarium waiting for me even before I spoke.

That Tuesday night we gathered at First Baptist Church along with more than 8,000 others. Dr. Hyles had declared the theme of the conference, "More Than Conquerors," and he had a number of folks on the program that evening.

Two precious Laotian young ladies told how they had seen their loved ones killed and how they had walked through jungles literally infested with dead bodies as they fled toward the waters and on to the boats that would help them escape communism and take them to freedom.

After they arrived in America, Dr. Hyles had taken them in and had allowed them to attend the high school there free of charge, as he had done for so many others who wanted a Christian education and true freedom that comes through knowing our Lord and Saviour Jesus Christ.

Next on the program was a young lady who had won more than a hundred souls to Christ, even though she was a paralytic and had to carry on her ministry from a wheelchair. After she gave her testimony, Dr. Hyles presented that young lady with a new electric wheelchair and a certificate to fly two weeks anywhere she wanted to go on United Airlines.

Then came Dr. and Mrs. Bob Kelley from Murfreesboro, Tennessee. Mrs. Kelley has multiple sclerosis; yet, Dr. Kelley has gone on and pastored a very large church—the Franklin Road

Baptist Church. Mrs. Kelley has stayed by his side, and he has stayed by hers; and their three lovely daughters are actively serving the Lord.

It was thrilling to hear their testimony and to hear them sing. Afterward Dr. Hyles presented Mrs. Kelley with a check for $1,000 for some new treatments that had been discovered for multiple sclerosis. He also had found out that she had always wanted a grandfather clock, and he presented her with one of the nicest ones I have ever seen.

Then came Dr. Bud Weniger, president of Maranatha Baptist Bible College. His wife was bedfast (also from multiple sclerosis) and could not be there, but he gave a testimony of God's grace that had seen them through Mrs. Weniger's illness and had enabled them to continue in the service of the Lord. After the testimony, Dr. Hyles told Dr. Weniger that he understood they were building a new home. He instructed Dr. Weniger to include in the house the things that would make life easier for Mrs. Weniger and to send the bill to the First Baptist Church of Hammond.

Dr. Hyles had deemed each one of these people more than conquerors and was truly an encouragement not only to *their* hearts, but also to the hearts of the people in the audience.

I had wept so much from hearing their stories that I was emotionally drained by the time Dr. Hyles said, "Now we are going to hear the story of Tom and Pam Williams."

Since it was so late in the evening when I went onto the platform, I whispered to Dr. Hyles, "How long do you want me to take?"

He answered, "You take as long as you need."

So for the next forty-five or fifty minutes, I told the story, "Twice Given"—the true story of our family's battle with death and our victory of love. We call it "Twice Given" because God gave Pam to me the first time in answer to my prayer for a wife after my first wife died, leaving me with a young son. He gave her to me a second time by delivering her from death's door, as I mentioned in the chapter entitled "Valley of the Shadow of Death."

As I told the story, if I remember correctly, we received five standing ovations. Then when I said, "Tim, will you please bring your mother to the platform," the auditorium almost vibrated with applause and praise to God as Pam stood and walked toward me.

Finally the crowd was quieted, and I had Pam answer some questions and do a few things that she could do. The people gave another standing ovation. Dr. Hyles and the folks in the audience were greatly touched by our story.

After we sat down, Dr. Hyles (who has traveled extensively and has spoken in some of the greatest coliseums and convention halls in the world) stood up and said, "This is the greatest moment of my entire ministry."

He continued, "To give an invitation would be foolish; the aisles of First Baptist would not contain the people that would come. You must do what I am going to do—get right with God right where you are."

And Dr. Hyles began to pray, "Lord, I've never been thankful that I could just walk to this pulpit; but tonight I am. Lord, I've never been thankful that when I lower my eyes, I can read and can understand what I read; but tonight I am . . . ." And he continued praying for quite some time, thanking God for so many things he had always taken for granted.

When he finished praying, Dr. Hyles turned to me and asked, "Brother Williams, how do you pay the nurse that you have with you tonight? Where do you get the money for her salary?"

I said, "We just believe God for it every month; and one way or another, it comes."

He turned to the audience and said, "Let's take an offering and give Brother Williams $10,000 to help him with his wife." After they passed the offering plates, Dr. Hyles turned to me and said, "I want you to come back in the morning and be on the platform at 8:30 a.m., and I'll present you with the offering in front of the people who gave it."

The next morning held more surprises. Completely unknown to me, Dr. Hyles had asked my children what they thought Pam would like, and they had told him a platform rocker. When we returned the next morning, he had his men bring up a beautiful rocker and present it to Pam. After she was seated, he asked me to come to the podium. Then he announced to me publicly, "We got a little more money last night than I thought we would get, and you are welcome to every cent of it. God bless you!" And he handed me a check for just over $38,000!

Needless to say, I was absolutely speechless, overwhelmed at the amazing love and concern of God's people. The crowd rose to their feet and gave a thunderous round of applause that must have lasted at least five minutes. Finally I was able to speak and thank them for the tremendous, unbelievable encouragement they had been to us.

Later my son Tim told me, "Dad, you'll never know what it meant for me to be here." And on two or three occasions since then, he has thanked me for asking him to share that special time in our lives. Of course, with that offering, I had plenty of money to pay his airplane ticket—and we didn't have to wait until the end of the month to pay it! I never would have forgiven myself if I had not exercised faith and gone on and invited him to see what God did and does for so many of His children in different ways.

With the money Dr. Hyles gave us, we were able to clear up a lot of debts and to get a fresh start in the ministry and in our own personal lives. We could never thank him and all the pastors enough for all they did for us that night.

Once again, God had manifested His blessings to encourage one of His servants along the pathway of life and had tremendously helped us face tomorrow.

10   More Blue Sky

To think that I would ever be invited to speak at Dr. Jack Hyles' Pastors' School was beyond my greatest expectations, so I felt deeply honored and grateful to God when asked to speak there in 1983. Then to be asked back in 1984 was almost more than I could believe.

In January, 1984 I had gone to Florida with some very close friends from Virginia—Dr. and Mrs. Bud Calvert and Colonel and Mrs. Aldon Guy. They were from the Fairfax Baptist Temple, the church that had stood by us so faithfully when my wife first became ill in 1978.

While in Florida, the Spirit of God very clearly impressed on my heart to call Dr. Hyles' secretary. When she answered the telephone, I asked, "Mrs. McKinney, have you been trying to reach me?"

She said, "Indeed, I have! I've called the Sword of the Lord and several other places, but no one knew where you were."

I said, "The Spirit of the Lord told me that you were trying to reach me."

She replied, "Dr. Hyles wants you to speak at Pastors' School again this year—once on Tuesday night to tell the story to the pastors like you did last year, then on Wednesday night at the Civic Center. So many come to the Pastors' School that there is not enough room in the auditorium for the regular church people, so Dr. Hyles is renting the Civic Auditorium for the members of First Baptist Church, and he wants you to speak there."

So in March, 1984, Mrs. Williams and I, along with the young lady who was caring for my wife, flew to Chicago, where we were again royally welcomed by one of Dr. Hyles' assistants.

Since our three youngest children had not been at Pastors' School the first time I shared the story of our testimony, I made arrangements for them to be there this time to see their daddy and mother honored and to see that in the darkest of valleys, God sends a light.

For Pastors' School each year, Dr. Hyles bases his theme on some word or event. The theme for the 1984 Pastors' School was based on the Olympics that were going on in our nation at that time. He took the events of the Olympics and made a spiritual application for each of them. In my case, he equated weight-lifting with burden-bearing.

For this particular night, Dr. Hyles also had invited two other men to speak who also had borne some tremendous burdens.

The first was Ron Hamilton. Although he lost one of his eyes as a result of cancer, he continues to serve the Lord in a tremendous way. He expressed his victory in Christ through the song, "Rejoice in the Lord," now so famous across the country. Ron refers to himself as "Patch the Pirate," and he and his lovely wife have a tremendous ministry in working with children as well as adults.

The second man on the program was Dr. Jack Hudson, pastor of the Northside Baptist Church in Charlotte, North Carolina. Dr. Hudson has one of the most severe arthritic conditions in his back that doctors have ever seen. He cannot so much as turn his neck. His dear wife Joyce has to put hot sandbags on his back each morning before he can get out of bed. His testimony was a terrific example of one who had endured great suffering for the glory of God and had gone on serving the Lord in a tremendous way.

By the time these two men finished, it was late in the evening. Yet, when Dr. Hyles called me to the platform, he told me to take all the time I needed to tell our story.

At the end, as Pam came to the platform, the audience responded just as they had the previous year, with almost unbelievable applause and a wonderful time of praising God.

Dr. Hyles was so deeply touched that he turned to the crowd and said, "Folks, I had not intended to take an offering tonight; in fact, there is not an offering plate in the building. But I believe the world ought to *see* this story—not just hear it. Let's help Brother Williams raise the money to put this story on film. You can pass your money to the aisles, and we will have men go up and down the aisles and collect the money and bring it to the communion table."

I wish everyone in the world could have been in that service. The men continued bringing money until it was, without exaggeration, two feet high on the communion table and was sliding onto the floor. Someone yelled, "Get a trash can!" A large drum was brought in, and the money half filled the drum.

The next night I spoke at the Civic Center to almost 6,500 of Dr. Hyles' church people while he continued at the Pastors' School with about 8,200.

It was snowing so hard in Hammond that we could hardly see to drive, but it didn't stop the people. After telling our story to his church people, they also received an offering for us.

Then for Thursday night, Dr. Hyles asked us to go back to the Pastors' School. In keeping with the Olympics theme, he put a gold medal around the neck of each person who had participated in the program that week, and then he asked the orchestra to play our favorite gospel song. Mine was, and still is, "God Leads His Dear Children Along."

As the orchestra played, I was reminded once again of God's faithfulness to lead His children. He leads some through the water, some through the flood, some through the fire, some through great sorrow; but He leads all of us through His precious blood and gives us a song—in the night seasons and all the day long. He really does help us face our tomorrows.

When the orchestra finished, Dr. Hyles asked us to come to the platform, and he presented us with a check for $50,000 to begin a film of our story. Again I was absolutely stunned and overwhelmed by his generosity and the generosity of the people. And again the Lord had done exceeding abundantly above anything we could have asked or imagined.

I knew that some of the people probably had given the last penny they had. I found out later that some of the pastors decided to fast the rest of the week and give us the money they had planned to use for food. How my heart was touched by the sacrificial spirit of the people!

When we returned home, I began looking for someone to film the story, not knowing even where to begin. After several months, God graciously led me to the folks at Olive's Film Productions in Huntsville, Alabama.

After talking with them and seeing their emphasis on doing quality work that would glorify the Lord, I knew in my heart they were the people God wanted to produce the movie, which we would call *Twice Given*.

The script-writer read my book, *Twice Given for God's Glory*, and listened to the story of our testimony on cassette several times during the next few weeks. After some modifications, we had the script that we believed God wanted us to use in producing this major motion picture.

We then began production of the film, but it was not long before the money ran out. We had completed only a nine-minute segment. Little had I realized when I started this project that it would cost so much money to produce such a film, but I thought we could raise the money to complete it.

I sent a letter to more than 14,000 churches, explaining about the need and asking them to consider helping with the costs, but we only received about $3,000 in response to that mailing. It was evident this was not the way God was going to supply the money.

By this time, I think a lot of people were beginning to wonder if I had misread the will of God and that He really did not want a film made of our story.

Several months passed, and we showed the nine-minute segment in various churches to encourage folks to give so the film could be completed. We received about $30,000 that way.

In June, 1985, I was in a revival service in the northeastern part of the United States. As I walked into the foyer of the church on Sunday morning, a man I had never met walked up to me and asked, "Aren't you Dr. Tom Williams?"

I replied, "Yes, I am."

He continued, "I've never met you; in fact, I've never heard you speak except on tape. Your testimony has blessed and changed my life, and I have been looking forward to meeting you. How is the film coming?"

"Nothing is happening on the film right now," I told him. "We're out of money."

He asked, "How much more do you need?"

At that time, I thought we needed only another $165,000; and that's what I told him. But I found out later that it would cost another $202,000, of which we had, at that time, about $30,000.

He told me, "I'll take care of $100,000 of that this morning."

I gasped, "Did you say *$100,000*?"

He replied, "Yes, I did."

I could hardly believe what he was saying! I wept profusely, overwhelmed at what God had done in touching this man's heart and in his obedience in listening to what God wanted in his life and in mine.

This godly man handed me a check that morning for $50,000, with a promise to send the other $50,000 over the next three months, which he did.

I immediately called David Olive, president of Olive's Film Productions, and told him about the $100,000, asking them to resume production on the film. I knew that, if God would send that much, He would send the rest.

In November, after we had used up the $100,000, another payment of $44,000 came due. We had $3,000 toward that payment, and another man sent $5,000, making a total of $8,000. We still lacked $36,000.

On the weekend before the payment was due, I was holding a meeting in a church in the northern part of the United States. I had shown the nine-minute segment and told the people about the additional money that was needed. After the service that Friday night, one of the men walked up to me and said he would like to take me to supper on Sunday night after the service.

At supper, he told me that he had a burden for the film but that God had not put a definite amount on his heart. He did not know what, if anything, he ought to do; he just knew he was burdened about it.

He and his wife went home that night and prayed. I also prayed that night in the motel. The next morning when we met for breakfast, I asked him, "How did you sleep last night?"

He answered, "Not very well. In fact, I didn't sleep much at all."

I told him, "I prayed that you would not be able to sleep, but that you would spend that time in prayer."

He replied, "Well, your prayer was answered."

I quizzed, "Did you reach a decision on how much you should give toward the film?"

In his quiet, gentle manner, he replied, "My wife and I always discuss big decisions like this, and I asked her what she thought we should give. She thought maybe $5,000. That was the amount I had in mind at first, but then I thought maybe we should give $10,000. But I really did not have any peace about that either. So we went to bed, not having any real peace about what we ought to do."

He continued, "I got up this morning and the Devil told me, 'Don't do anything.' But I knew that was not right. I began to read, by the leading of the Spirit of God, from the book of Proverbs, chapter 3. I read verses 5 and 6—'Lean not unto thine own understanding. In all thy ways acknowledge him, and he shall direct thy paths'—and kept on reading. The Lord spoke to my heart through verses 27 and 28: 'Withhold not good from them to whom it is due, when it is in the power of thine hand to do it. Say not unto thy neighbour, Go, and come again, and tomorrow I will give; when thou hast it by thee.'"

He looked across the table at me and said, "That's pretty plain, isn't it, preacher!"

I replied, "Yes, Sir, it is."

He smiled, "Well, relax and enjoy your breakfast. We'll drive out to the plant afterwards, and I will write a check for $36,000 to the Tom Williams Evangelistic Ministries for this payment on the film."

I don't have to tell you that again I was overwhelmed by the goodness of God and His people. It sure made the plane flight home a lot easier that day, because the very next day I had to face David Olive—with or without the money. How I praised God that I was able to make the complete payment when it was due!

As David and I viewed what had been filmed, we realized

we would not be able to leave out enough of it to stay within the sixty-minute limit, as agreed upon in our contract, and still do justice to the story. After omitting all we felt we could omit, it was still almost eighty minutes long, which would add considerably to the cost. Finally David and I agreed on a price for the extra minutes. Including the balance owed on the original contract and the extra minutes, we would need $32,000 more by the time the film was released the following month.

The producers were working feverishly to complete the film to send to churches in time for their New Year's Eve service. When I broke the news to David that we needed the film completed in time for the premiere showing in early December, he said they would do their best.

I had talked to Dr. Hyles about his having the premiere showing at First Baptist Church, which he gladly agreed to do. With his busy schedule that time of year, and since he wanted the students of Hyles-Anderson College to see it before they went home for Christmas vacation, we chose the date of Sunday night, December 8.

I received the film on December 7, and several members of my family, along with some friends, flew up to Chicago, where Dr. Hyles' assistant met us and escorted us to our hotel. The next evening, we watched the movie with very mixed emotions. On one hand, we were saddened as we saw Pam portrayed as she had been before her illness, and then again as we relived the events of her illness. On the other hand, we were grateful that God had provided the means for the story to be put on film so countless thousands of people could be encouraged to trust the Lord and see Him miraculously answer prayer, regardless of circumstances.

Dr. Hyles had asked his people to come early that night so we could start the film at 5:45 p.m. This would leave time for him to preach afterward. There were probably 8,000 people present for the premiere of *Twice Given*.

At various times during the film, the people openly praised the Lord and applauded; many of them wept. As the film ended, the people joyously gave a thunder of applause and honored us with a standing ovation. They gave another standing ovation later when I asked Pam to join me on the platform. We all rejoiced together at what God had done in her life.

Dr. Hyles was greatly impressed by the quality of production and by the story itself, and he asked me how much we needed to finish paying for the film. When I told him, he turned to the audience and said, "Folks, Brother Williams needs $32,000 more to pay for the film. I think he has suffered enough and has sacrificed enough. He does not have that kind of money, so it is up to us—the folks here tonight—to make this payment."

That night, Dr. Hyles raised the $32,000 and gave us a cashier's check the next morning before we left for home.

A miracle made possible the story of *Twice Given*, and God in His sovereignty had seen fit to perform another miracle in providing the money to produce a film so the story could continue touching the hearts and lives of countless thousands of people throughout America and throughout the world. Truly, another tomorrow had been victoriously faced by the grace of our all-sufficient Lord.

11   Eight Precious Jewels

This book would not have been complete without paying tribute to eight precious jewels for the tremendous weight they lifted, for the blessing they have been, and for the encouragement they have brought to my heart in helping me face my tomorrows.

As I mentioned in an earlier chapter, when our oldest daughter married, we did not have anyone to help with Pam when I had to be away.

We prayed and asked the Lord's guidance in hiring a nurse— someone who could help care for Pam, do some of the housework, and travel with us to my evangelistic meetings.

God so wonderfully provided the helper we needed then and has continued to send someone as the various nurses have married or moved on to other areas of ministry.

During the next few years, God brought us seven young ladies who have been and continue to be precious jewels in our lives. Had these ladies not been willing to give a portion of their lives to meet such a tremendous need in our family, it would have been physically impossible for me to do everything I felt God wanted me to do.

How thankful I am for their parents' willingness to let them come and help take care of one of God's dear servants!

Each of the nurses is like a jewel. Each one has a different radiance, bringing rays of joy into our lives and our home. Even though I have tried in many ways to express my appreciation,

I could never thank them enough for the investment they have made into our lives.

Jewel Number 1

The first nurse, Janice Williams, a young lady in her twenties, came to work for us about a week before Phyllis married. As I mentioned in an earlier chapter, Janice came to us from Kansas City as a direct answer to prayer. She traveled with us, lived with us, shared in the work, helped take care of Pam and was such a help.

Most of the girls learned to cook after they started working for us. So their coming not only helped us tremendously, but the experience they gained helped prepare them to be better wives.

I told each of the girls that I did not want her to think of her work merely as a job but as a ministry. I knew if they didn't consider it a ministry, they would not stay; caring for an invalid takes real dedication. Since they were going to be living with us, I wanted each to feel like a daughter to us and let us be like a second mom and dad to her.

I had told Janice that, if she would come and work for us, I would pray every day that God would send her a husband! She wanted so much to be married and to be a good wife and mother. I faithfully prayed every day, asking God to bring into her life the young man of His choice.

A few months later we were in Emporia, Kansas for a meeting. After the pastor had checked us into the motel and we had made sure Pam was comfortable, I said to Janice, "Janice, this is where you are going to meet your husband."

She replied, "Oh, Brother Williams! Don't tease about that!"

But I told her, "I am not teasing. The Holy Spirit spoke to my heart and told me this is where you are going to meet your husband."

I knew without doubt that God had impressed this on my heart, and it was such a blessing to know He was going to answer my prayers.

We began the meeting, and on Sunday night a young man came forward and told the pastor God had called him to preach. And what a fine young man he was!

Later that evening as I glanced back toward the tape and book table where Janice was working, I noticed Greg hanging around the table like a bee around a hive. He was doing the same thing the second night, too.

I walked by and jokingly said, "Either buy something or ask Janice out—one or the other!"

His face turned red and he sputtered, "W-w-well, I *was* trying to get up the nerve to ask her out!"

They dated a couple of times that week, and the hook was set. Soon after we got back home, Greg called her. Then he sent her a letter . . . and another one. Then he came to see her. Several months later Janice Williams became Mrs. Greg Steiner.

A lot of people said, "Dr. Williams, you just prayed yourself out of a nurse."

I replied, "Yes, but how thrilling to know that we could be a blessing to Janice, as she was such a blessing to us!"

Greg and Janice now live in Michigan, where Greg is pursuing his pastoral calling. They are serving the Lord and have three wonderful children.

I will never forget the day I walked into my office when Janice was still working with us and found on my desk a letter from her, saying, "Dr. Williams, I have often wondered if preachers live what they preach. After living with your family for these months, you are one I do not wonder about anymore."

That letter meant more to me than any introduction I could ever receive in public speaking or anywhere else. Janice had lived with us and traveled with us. She had seen us in all circumstances. And that was her testimony of our life and ministry. I thank God that she felt that way!

May God bless you, Janice, as you go on for Him today, serving the Lord as Greg's wife, the children's mother and a dear servant of our Saviour!

Jewel Number 2

The second jewel was Karin Swinehart, a young lady from Pennsylvania. Karin was a senior in high school when we met her. Again we recognized the sovereignty of God in the way He arranged for us to meet and later to work out the details for her coming to live with us.

The week we met Karin, Janice was off for a week, and I was taking care of Pam by myself. Although I could do her hair, I knew it would save me a lot of time if someone else did it. So I made an announcement in the church where I was preaching that week that I would like for someone to do Pam's hair.

A teenage girl walked up to me after the service and said, "I am studying cosmetology in high school, and I would be happy to do your wife's hair."

And Karin did an excellent job of caring for Mrs. Williams' hair all that week.

During the week, Karin mentioned that her sister Kathy, who was graduating from college as a medical secretary, wanted to work in Denver, Colorado. Since we were living in Denver at the time, I knew several doctors there and felt that one of them might need a good secretary. I told Kathy that, if she would like to go to Denver, she could stay with us until she could find a job. I told her parents I did not feel it was good for a young lady to live alone in a large city like Denver. Her parents appreciated our offer and felt secure, knowing their daughter was living with someone they trusted.

As a graduation gift to Karin, Mr. and Mrs. Swinehart paid

her way to Denver so she could stay with Kathy for awhile.

During the next few days, I introduced Kathy to several doctors, and one of them hired her to be his secretary. It was a joy to know that God had again used us to be a blessing in a young person's life.

While they lived with us, Karin so wonderfully took care of Pam, just like she would have had she been working for us. Janice would be leaving soon, and I felt that Karin would make an excellent replacement.

With this thought in mind, I approached Karin and quizzed her as to her goals in life. She answered, "I have always had a deep desire to help older folks and to help folks with illnesses."

I replied, "I realize you are very young, but would you like to have the job of taking care of Mrs. Williams?"

She said she really believed she would be interested but that she would need to talk to her parents before making a commitment. I agreed.

Karin's folks were not opposed to her taking the job, and she was such a blessing! Karin had much understanding for such a young girl, and she had a desire to help me and my wife.

As I said before, the blessing was a two-way street. Before Pam's illness, God had given me the ability to coordinate colors and to suggest hair styles, clothing and jewelry that looked nice together. In fact, I bought all of Pam's clothing, and she constantly received compliments on the way she looked and dressed. After she became ill, it really was not a burden for me to buy the things she needed and to keep her looking nice.

Since the young ladies who helped us were such a blessing, I tried to be a blessing in return by buying them some clothes from time to time and giving suggestions on coordinates, jewelry, hair styles and other things.

I will never forget what Karin's parents told me in a letter after she went back home: "Brother Williams, we sent you a little high school girl; you returned to us a fine young lady."

I worked at helping the girls grow up and be what God wanted them to be in every way. Of course, living with us twenty-four hours a day, they saw my prayer life and my Bible study life. They heard me preach almost every night. And the girls learned to pray. I am not saying they didn't already pray, but they learned to pray for longer periods of time by broadening their burden for people and their trials. What a tremendous blessing it was to see them grow spiritually!

Karin left us to attend Maranatha Baptist Bible College. She later met a young man and fell in love. Karin was married in October, 1987.

Karin, may God richly bless you. Please know that you hold a very special place in our hearts.

Jewel Number 3

The third jewel was Becky Hudson, a young woman in her early twenties. Becky was born and reared in the state of Michigan. We met her at Maranatha Baptist Bible College in Wisconsin. I was speaking there shortly before Karin left us, and I had made an announcement from the pulpit that we were seeking the will of God in hiring a young lady to replace Karin. That week Becky very nervously came and spoke to me about the job. She said she was graduating and that she had extensive experience from working in a nursing home.

After talking with Becky and with the faculty and administrators at the college, I felt that she was the one God wanted to help take care of my dear wife. Becky was an answer to prayer, as we had prayed that God would send us a young person from that particular Bible college.

Some people have said, "Brother Williams, it seems that many young ladies would be interested in the job because they get to travel so much and see so many places."

I can see that would be true in a sense, but what most people do not realize is that caring for my wife is a big job, and it is not always easy. Pam is not always pleasant—not because she chooses to be unpleasant, but because of her mental condition. And to take care of someone else's body in all the bodily functions of a woman is not exactly enjoyable.

And, of course, the rigors of travel are devastating, considering how much we are gone. It means the nurse has to get up early, get herself and Mrs. Williams dressed, do their hair, the laundry, pack for the trip, then spend twenty-four hours a day with Mrs. Williams.

The days we are home, the nurse has much of the responsibility for cleaning house and preparing the meals. I help with much of the work and the shopping, but she still handles most of it.

I am not saying that it is not a blessing for the girls to do these things; it is. But it is also very strenuous on them.

And Becky did a good job. Her experience in caring for invalids was a rich blessing, and it wonderfully prepared her to take care of my wife.

Becky was living with us when God spoke to my heart about moving from Denver, Colorado, where we had lived for sixteen years, to Murfreesboro, Tennessee.

She and my daughter Penny (then sixteen) stayed at home one week to pack our household things, and I took Pam with me. When we returned from the week-long meeting, Becky and Penny had everything ready to put on the big moving van. Of course, this kind of work really was not in Becky's "job description," but I never once heard her complain.

Just as we had finished loading the moving van, I remembered that a neighbor who lived about a mile and a half from us had borrowed some things and I had forgotten to stop by and pick them up.

Since I still had to load the horses and get the pickup truck ready, I asked Penny to drive to the neighbor's house and get the things, instructing her to be very careful, since it had started to snow and the ground was freezing.

Penny went over and got the things and was almost back home when the car began skidding. She lost control and collided with another car, doing almost $8,000 damage to our new automobile.

God miraculously spared Penny and protected her and the person in the other car from injury, for which we were so grateful.

We had planned to follow the moving van to Tennessee. Becky, Penny and Pam would go in the car, and I would follow with the pickup and horse trailer. But since the car was wrecked, we all had to ride in the pickup. I was grateful it had a dual cab, but it still was hard on Pam to travel so far in a truck.

Since we had been delayed in leaving, I called the realtor in Tennessee and arranged for someone to meet the moving van. Thank God, our realtor, Clayton Rutledge, a wonderful Christian man, made arrangements for the truck to be unloaded at the house we had purchased from him. What a tremendous blessing that was to us!

The trip to Tennessee was long and tiring; but again, Becky was so sweet about it all. We later had a lot of laughs about some of the problems experienced while Becky was with us.

I thank God for bringing Becky into our lives and for using us in her life. Becky's mother was a Christian when we met her, but she was out of fellowship with the Lord. Through our ministry, her mother got right with God and began to live for Christ. As a result, Becky's father got saved. What a thrill to know that her mother is right with the Lord and that her dad is on his way to Heaven!

Becky's college degree was in elementary education, so the real desire of her heart was to be a teacher. Becky and I talked it over, and we both agreed that she should pursue her career. I introduced her to Dr. Bud Calvert of the Fairfax Baptist Temple in Fairfax, Virginia, and she was hired to teach in the elementary school, where she has been for several years.

May God richly bless and keep you, Becky, as you continue to walk in the ways of the Lord.

Jewel Number 4

The fourth precious jewel that came to us was mined by the hand of God from Des Moines, Iowa. I was speaking in the Grandview Park Baptist Church, where my good friend, Orlan Wilhite, is pastor.

I had shared with him our need for someone who would come and live with us and take care of Mrs. Williams. He told me of several young ladies in the church and particularly one family who had three lovely daughters, all sold out to Christ, as was the whole family.

Pastor Wilhite later introduced me to the oldest girl, Pennie Graber. After talking with Pennie for more than an hour, I was so impressed with her spirituality and desire to do the will of God that I told her I would like to talk to her parents about the possibility of having her work with us.

Even though Pennie was just graduating from high school, I felt she could do the job and would be an asset to our life and ministry.

After meeting with Mr. and Mrs. Loren Graber, they gave permission for Pennie to travel with us and take care of Pam.

Pennie went through some tremendous pressures when she first came to us. Some of the folks in the Des Moines area felt she was out of the will of God in leaving her family, her church and her ministry there.

One of the things that had impressed me about this young lady was that she had the largest bus route in her church—a church that really is aggressive and does a tremendous job for the glory of God. But even though she missed her family, friends and church, she felt God wanted her to help in our ministry.

Pennie was an unusual girl in a number of ways. After she gave up her bus route to work with us, she wrote a personal letter to every child on her bus route every month. She also wrote to many other folks. While she was with us, she averaged writing 150 letters per month. It was so precious to see her diligence.

Pennie was the first young lady to work with us who had the same first name as one of our family members. This was a little confusing to my dear wife—to have two in the house with the same name. But after awhile, Pam found a way of making it known which one she was speaking to, making it a little less confusing to her.

Pennie fit right in with our family, but she missed her folks so very much. It was our privilege one day to surprise her by flying her mother to Tennessee to spend some time with her. On another occasion, the entire Graber family came to a camp where I was preaching, and we had some wonderful fellowship with them.

Pennie would pull little pranks and do other things to keep life interesting. One day we had an idea. (I say we because I do not think either of us would have dared admit that we thought of it alone!)

While the Grabers were at the camp, we were enjoying, among other things, the big water slide. Mrs. Graber, a very lovely lady, had gone down the slide and was just coming up out of the water when we took her picture. She had on a tee shirt and culottes, and her hair was all wet and tousled from the water, giving her a "drowned rat" look.

It really was mean of us, but we had that picture enlarged to poster size and presented it to Mr. Graber for Christmas. Even today, when we see the Grabers, the big poster is a popular conversation piece.

In December, 1984, Pennie went back to Des Moines for Christmas. While there, God began to make a dream come true for her. Before Pennie came to work for us, she had secretly admired one of the single young men in her church. Since he was several years older than Pennie, he had not asked her for a date.

Maybe it was a matter of "absence makes the heart grow fonder," for he did express an interest in Pennie during the holidays, and they began to date.

It seemed that Dennis Carroll might be just the one God had brought into Pennie's life as an answer to our prayers for the right man, even though I had not expected it so soon.

When Pennie came back to work after Christmas, seemingly all she could talk about was Dennis, Dennis, Dennis!

In February, while we were in Memphis, Tennessee, for a meeting, I asked, "Pennie, how would you like to go home?"

Tears of joy welled up in her eyes. She asked, "For how many days?"

I replied, "From now on. You are no good to us anymore; all you can think about is Dennis, Dennis, Dennis!"

Of course, I was joking when I said she was no longer any good to us. She was; she was precious. But I could see that returning home and getting to know Dennis better was God's will and that her heart was totally in Des Moines, Iowa.

Pennie returned home, and she and Dennis were married on August 31, 1985. It was my privilege to take part in the wedding ceremony for Pennie, as I had also done for Janice when she got married.

I thank God that Pennie is happily married and going on with Christ as a diligent worker in the Grandview Park Baptist Church.

Dennis and Pennie have a young son and are expecting another bundle of joy in the near future.

God bless you, Pennie. You hold a daughter's place in our hearts.

Jewel Number 5

The fifth precious jewel was Dawn Brown, a young girl from Kansas. Being highly recommended by one of our staff members, Dawn came to us on the spur of the moment. We had never met her, and she had never met us. Many years earlier her folks had heard me preach, and they knew about our ministry.

Dawn was only sixteen, but she was mature for her age and was going to school by correspondence because of the situation where they lived.

With her parents' blessings, she came to work with us on a three-month trial basis. I really had some doubts that a girl so young could do the job, but Dawn did do a good job. She had worked one summer in a nursing home, and that experience really helped her in Pam's situation. Dawn so wonderfully met our needs in taking care of Pam and helping in our home.

Dawn was the first young lady to work for us who did not know how to drive. Even though we fly to most of our meetings, it is a big help to have someone go into town for things and take Pam to the shopping mall so she does not have to sit in the house all day. Before my wife became ill, she always liked to go shopping; although she no longer is able to shop for herself, she likes to go.

Since Dawn could not drive and since I felt she needed to be at home the last few years of her teen life, finish her schooling and be under her parents' influence, we felt it would be best for her to return home after the three months. I talked to Dawn not long ago, and she told me she is a good driver now.

God bless you, Dawn, as you go on with the Lord, serving Him and living for Him. And please know that we are praying for you, as for the other girls, that God's will shall be done in your life each day.

Jewel Number 6

The sixth young lady that God brought to us in the string of precious jewels was Lori Hennessey, also from Kansas. I had met Lori when I was preaching in Kansas. Her father runs a Christian camp there, and their family loves the Lord and serves Him with all their heart.

God's timing is always perfect, and He is orderly in everything He does. Dawn flew with us to Kansas City and her folks met us at the church to take her home. Mr. and Mrs. Hennessey brought Lori to the church the same night. So Lori started working for us the same night Dawn left. God had again answered prayer in a unique way, sending another young lady into our lives to help with Pam.

Lori was a student at Bob Jones University, majoring in physical education. She came to work for us the summer before her senior year. Lori's vivacious spirit was a real blessing and encouragement to both Pam and me.

I am also indebted to this young lady for helping me. I run a lot; and in my attempt to keep myself physically fit, I was running improperly, actually bringing on chest pains. Lori taught me to run correctly.

So many times when I am jogging, I thank God for Lori Hennessey and for her input into our lives.

Lori went back to Bob Jones University in the fall and finished college. She is now serving the Lord as a Christian schoolteacher in the Atlanta, Georgia, area.

Lori, from Mrs. Williams and me, let me say, "God bless you

and give you the husband and place of service He wants for your life."

Jewel Number 7

The seventh jewel was Pam Alcorn, daughter of one of the pastor's assistants in our home church in Murfreesboro, Tennessee.

Pam had attended college the year before she started working with us, but she did not feel it was God's will for her to return the next year. She needed a job and, since we needed someone to take Lori's place, the Lord wonderfully led us together.

Pam's having the same first name as my wife sometimes created a point of confusion in Mrs. Williams' mind, but she adjusted well, pointing out that Pam Alcorn was "a *different* Pam."

We are so thankful that God brought this tiny jewel into our lives. Pam is by far the smallest of any of the girls. Because of her size, she was concerned that she might not be able to do the work. But as someone has well said, "It's not the size of the man in the fight; it's the size of the fight in the man that makes the difference."

Pam proved that her size was not really a problem, as she so willingly gave herself to the rigors of travel and all the responsibilities that go along with taking care of my wife.

Pam has done a terrific job of caring for and loving Mrs. Williams and being a blessing to my own heart as well.

Because of some serious physical problems which "little Pam" had, someone said to me, "Dr. Williams, with all the burdens you already carry with your wife, it doesn't seem right that you should also have to go through the burdens of having a nurse with so many physical problems."

I replied, "Maybe God felt that this young lady needed real understanding and is allowing me the privilege of being a blessing and encouragement to her, as she is to me and my wife."

Pam had tumors in different parts of her body and it seemed, from all indications, that she had cancer. There are five symptoms of a certain kind of cancer, and Pam had all five. We prayed earnestly and sought the Lord concerning her problem. She went to the doctor. A series of tests were all negative; there was no sign of malignancy. We rejoiced over God's goodness and His answer to our prayers.

My, how good and how great our God is! We are so thrilled that Mr. and Mrs. Dan Alcorn did such a terrific job rearing their daughter to be a soul winner, to love the Word of God, and to desire to be in the center of His will.

Many times Pam has said, "Dr. Williams, I know I am doing what God wants me to do."

Jewel Number 8

The eighth jewel is a widow, Cathleen Mays. Mrs. Mays is seventy years old and is a rare jewel indeed.

For about two years she came to our home while we were in town between meetings. She did most of the cooking and much of the housework. She was a real blessing to all of us in so many ways.

Mrs. Mays is an old-fashioned type of cook, in that everything she cooks is delicious. The nurses really appreciated her being there. It not only lightened their workload, but we all tremendously enjoyed her cooking.

Mrs. Mays spent hours with my wife, reading to her and playing Scrabble and other games with her. She was so patient to tell Pam what word to spell, then to show her how the letters should be placed to spell the word.

I was so glad to be able to take Mrs. Mays to Hawaii with us in 1985 and, in some small way, show our appreciation for all she meant to us.

Mrs. Mays, you are one of the godliest women I know. I take

this opportunity to publicly say thank you for all you have meant and do mean to us.

Thank you, girls and Mrs. Mays, for all the memories we have shared. In laughter and in tears. In quoting Scripture and in prayer. Thank you for the blessings you have all brought into our lives. I trust that I will always be a blessing to you and your families. Truly, you have been a vital part of our lives in helping us face our tomorrows.

12 | God's Ways Are Not Our Ways

I suppose I have been asked literally thousands of times, "Dr. Williams, will Pam ever be well? Will she ever be the same as she was before her illness?"

I do not know the answers to those questions because, as this chapter title indicates, God's ways are not our ways. If I could have had my way, Pam would have been healed at the very onset of her illness.

Even though I like to think that I was surrendered to the will of God and wanted His will in my life, I am sure that in the deep recesses of my heart, my most earnest cry in that hour was, "God, please heal Pam!"

But God in His sovereignty and wisdom knew what He wanted and what He was doing. Her being snatched from the clutches of death is not the only miracle that has taken place in our lives. God also worked a miracle in breaking and tenderizing my own heart.

I remember something Dr. Lee Roberson said while he was pastoring Highland Park Baptist Church in Chattanooga, Tennessee. After I had told our story in the chapel service at Tennessee Temple University, Dr. Roberson stood and said, "Ladies and gentlemen, I marvel at the miracle God has worked in Mrs. Williams' life . . . but an equal miracle has been wrought in Tom Williams' heart."

Dr. Roberson's statement was true. God has given me a heart to understand the pains and sufferings of others, to identify with and encourage those who are passing through very, very deep trials.

Some walk through the night of testing very quickly; some people's valleys are very short. Our trial has lasted several years. Somehow it seems that we are better able to console and encourage the hearts of the weary and heavy laden now than we were in the earlier years of the trial.

I have learned that Christians need not be surprised or alarmed when God does not change our circumstances or remove our trial. His own dear Son walked in a valley all the way from the cradle to the cross. No wonder the Scripture says we have a High Priest who is touched with the feelings of our infirmities, One who faced temptations just like you and I face . . . yet, He did not yield to sin.

I am so thankful today that the Lord Jesus Christ is the Great Comforter who comforts our hearts and enables us to comfort others. It would be impossible to include all the reports we have heard of how God has used the story of our testimony.

Someone gave a copy of our book, *Twice Given for God's Glory*, to a young mother who had been told she had severe cancer and did not have long to live. She read the book and was so encouraged that she decided to get out of bed and go on serving the Lord as long as she could. This lady later said, "The book was such an encouragement that it gave me strength to go on for these two years to serve Christ and to take care of my family. I am sure that I do not have much longer to live; the doctor has found another mass. But I will live for the Lord as long as I draw breath. I wanted to thank you for writing and living *Twice Given*."

Similar stories come from all over America, and I praise the Lord for His goodness to us in our trial.

God has also done a wonderful work in my children's lives. They have been used by God to set an example to so many other young people whose parents have experienced affliction. We are so thankful that God's ways are not our ways and His thoughts are not our thoughts.

If God had stopped the story in those early days of the trial, there would have been no best-selling book called *Twice Given for God's Glory*—a book that has been so mightily used by God. There would have been no story to tell at Dr. Hyles' Pastors' School. There would have been no film to carry the story and the title *Twice Given*.

Many believe that *Twice Given* is the greatest Christian film ever produced. I am so grateful for the letters and telephone calls telling of lives changed, homes restored, marriages cemented and souls saved.

After reading the book or seeing the movie, some couples have told me they had not realized how sweet a marriage could be, how much they could love each other, how giving God intended for them to be. They were so thankful for a second chance to make a go of their marriage, grateful that both of them were in good health.

If the Lord had stopped the story any earlier, there would have been no phone call from Dr. James Dobson's secretary, asking if they could run our story on their nationwide *Focus on the Family* radio program.

I was told that several million people heard the story, aired in December, 1985, and again in May, 1986, under the title, "Loving My Wife Back to Health."

In a personal letter, Dr. Dobson said, "Tom, it is incredible to see what God does with your story."

One of his staff members told me that they received a greater response from our program than they had received from any other program up to that point. We also received many letters and telephone calls.

Near the close of the program, Dr. Dobson asked me two

questions—questions I hear everywhere I go: "What is Pam's condition now?" and, "What if she never gets well?"

To answer the first question, my wife is probably on the level of a second-grade child insofar as her reading and understanding are concerned. Although Pam expresses practically no emotions, she is very much like a child. She looks to me for total security. If I am with her, she is happy; if I am not with her, she is unhappy. Therefore, we are seldom apart.

It takes a tremendous amount of work to travel with Pam and take care of her in all the different situations we face. At each motel room, she has to adjust her thinking to where the bathroom is located, since she gets up two or three times during the night, waking me each time either to tell me she is going to the bathroom or to ask permission to go.

For several months it seemed God had healed her of seizures; then He allowed them to come again. During one of the seizures, she fell backward and hit her head on a dresser. We have to make sure that someone is with her twenty-four hours a day. Although the seizures can happen at any time, we are grateful that she does not have them very often.

I thank God that Pam eats and sleeps well. And, as far as we know, she is physically healthy. She enjoys life as much as she possibly can in her situation. It is a blessing to hear her laugh and to bring joy to so many thousands across the nation as she joins in singing hymns—not because she remembers them from before her illness, but from having memorized them as they were sung night after night in the various churches where I have preached since she awoke from the coma. So many folks have commented that the radiance of her face is so sweet and such a blessing to them.

After the services, Pam sits and waits for me like a child would wait for her father. She calls me "Honey, Sir."

Question Number 2

The second question Dr. Dobson asked me was, "What if she never gets well?"

I replied, "Sir, it doesn't make any difference. I am committed to her for life."

I am so thankful to God for His sovereignty and wisdom as He continues to allow our trial. Although there are many things we do not understand, I realize that God—not man—is in control. The very fact that God has not chosen to heal my wife or to take her on to Heaven means that He still has a purpose for our present situation. He will not prolong the trial one day beyond what is necessary to accomplish His will.

It is my prayer that as people read the book, watch the movie, or hear me tell the story of our testimony, they will realize there is no way that Tom Williams, a mere man, could ever have done all I have done for my wife except through Him.

In myself, I do not have the strength to face tomorrow. But I am empowered by a strength beyond myself—the power of Almighty God, the One who knows what suffering is all about. May all praise and glory go to our Heavenly Father, the Lord Jesus Christ, and the blessed Holy Spirit. Truly, the great Trinity of Heaven sustained me through the years of loneliness, brokenheartedness and tears.

May you also look to God for strength to face your tomorrows. . .and may you be changed for *His* glory!

For a complete list of books available from the Sword of the Lord, write to Sword of the Lord Publishers, P. O. Box 1099, Murfreesboro, Tennessee 37133.